# Please Don't Drink

*from the*

# Finger Bowl!®

Pat Mayfield

# Please Don't Drink

## *from the*

# Finger Bowl!®

*A Guide to Business Protocol*

Fifth Printing 2013

## Pat Mayfield

www.patmayfield.com

Pat Mayfield Consulting, LLC
PO Box 10095
Pleasanton, CA 94588

Published by Insight Publishing
647 Wall Street
Sevierville, TN 37862

Fifth Printing 2013

Printed in the United States of America.

978-1-60013-020-5 eBook ISBN
978-1-60013-199-8 Hard Copy ISBN

Cover by Steve Wilson

Photography by Chuck Mayfield

Illustrations by Chet Molzen and John Trefethen

*Please Don't Drink from the Finger Bowl!*®
is offered as general information only.
Portions of text from Manners for Success® are
included in *Please Don't Drink from the Finger Bowl!*®

*This book is dedicated to Carol Sofranac,*
*who opened this door of opportunity.*

A special thanks for their advice, help,
and encouragement of the *Manners for Success*® series
and *Please Don't Drink from the Finger Bowl!*® goes to:

Chuck Mayfield, Karen Mayfield, Eric Turner,

Lee and Misty Tyree, Millicent Wasell,

Ron Robinson, Terry Jones, Kay Paumier,

Rene Siegel, Jim and Pamela Ott, Carol Keane,

Rick Babick, Tess Collins, Judy Wheeler Ditter,

Frank O'Connor, Shelley Powers, Tina Butts,

Vicki Fullenkamp, Susie Anderson,

Michelle Coughlin, Megan Huffman, Michelle Kappie,

Bruce Ruthven, Rosemarie Demonte,

Elizabeth Hamrick, Maynette and David Briethraup,

Judy and Dennis Matthies, Dr. Lisa Weaver,

Livermore Valley Winegrowers Association,

Jan Hunter, Teresa Jackson, Shirley Anderson,

Dr. Nelson Shelton, Lorraine Lambert,

Ben Servino, Dr. Sonjia Redmond, Judy and Paul Pettersen,

Suzanne Rudisill, and Sharon Davis.

*…and a very special thanks to*

*Desmond P. Smith for the inspiration of the cover,*
*and to*
*Jeanne Baach of Insight Publishing*
*for her encouragement and support*
*throughout this process.*

v

# TABLE OF CONTENTS

HOW TO GET THE MOST FROM THIS BOOK..............................................................x

WHY PROTOCOL ....................................................................................... X–XII

### SECTION I:  BUSINESS PROTOCOL

A. NETWORKING......... ................................................................1–14

    CAREER AND BUSINESS CARDS.............................................5-6, 11-12

    SYSTEM ...................................................................................... 6–9

    OVERCOMING SHYNESS ................................................................. 9

    THE HANDSHAKE...................................................................... 10

    INTRODUCTIONS...................................................................... 13

    REMEMBERING NAMES.............................................................. 14

B. BUSINESS COMMUNICATIONS .................................................. 15–24

    TELEPHONE.......................................................................... 16–18

    CELL PHONE ........................................................................... 19

    E-MAIL ............................................................................... 20–22

    THANK YOU NOTES ............................................................... 23–24

C. GENERAL BUSINESS MEETINGS................................................ 25–28

    GUIDELINES....................................................................... 25–28

    NAME BADGES...................................................................... 28

D. BUSINESS CASUAL DRESS ....................................................... 29–36

### SECTION II:  DINING PROTOCOL

A. THE TABLE ........................................................................ 37–40

B. PLACE SETTINGS AND CONDIMENTS........................................... 41–53

    DINNERWARE, FLATWARE, AND STEMWARE................................. 42–50

    NAPKINS .............................................................................. 51

    CONDIMENTS ..................................................................... 52–53

C. DINING STYLES AND SERVICE ................................................. 55–62

    AMERICAN AND CONTINENTAL STYLES ...................................... 56–57

    THE COURSES ............................................................ 58-59, 61-62

THE FINGER BOWL .................................................................. 60

D. THE BEVERAGE ................................................................... 63–70

WINE AND WINE TEST .......................................................... 64–68

THE TOAST ............................................................................ 69–70

E. BUSINESS ENTERTAINING .......................................................... 71–96

THE ROLE OF THE HOST AND THE GUEST ......................................... 72

GENERAL GUIDELINES AND MANNERS ...................................... 72–82, 85–89, 92–96

THE VEGETARIAN ...................................................................... 75

THE HOSTESS GIFT ................................................................ 79–80

SEATING ARRANGEMENT ........................................................ 82–84

CONVERSATION .................................................................... 89–91

SECOND SERVINGS AND DOGGIE BAGS .................................... 91–92, 93

PAYING THE BILL ........................................................... 94, 117, 136

F. CHALLENGING FOODS – GENERAL ............................................... 97–104

APPETIZERS ............................................................................ 98

BREAD AND ROLLS .................................................................. 99

COCKTAILS .......................................................................... 100

RELISHES ............................................................................. 101

SALADS ............................................................................... 102

SOUP ............................................................................. 103–104

G. CHALLENGING FOODS – SPECIFIC ............................................. 105–114

ARTICHOKES – CHICKEN .......................................................... 106

CORNISH HEN ....................................................................... 107

CORN ON THE COB – MEAT ...................................................... 108

OLIVES – SANDWICHES ............................................................ 109

SEAFOOD ............................................................................ 110

SORBET – SPAGHETTI ............................................................. 111

SUSHI ........................................................................... 112–113

CHOPSTICKS ........................................................................ 114

H. TIPPING ........................................................................ 115–120

## SECTION III: FREQUENTLY ASKED QUESTIONS

### ACCESSORIES

PURSES ....................................................................................................... 122

SATCHELS AND BRIEFCASES............................................................................ 122

WRITING IMPLEMENTS.................................................................................... 123

WHEN TO REPLACE......................................................................................... 123

### ANXIETY

CONQUERING SOCIAL ANXIETY ......................................................................... 124

TALKING WITH EXECUTIVES ............................................................................. 125

### CHAIRS

PUSHING IN THE CHAIR .................................................................................... 126

WHEN TO HELP ............................................................................................. 126

WHERE TO SIT .............................................................................................. 126

### CLOTHING

SUITS, SPORTS COATS, AND BLAZERS................................................................ 127

REMOVING THE JACKET ............................................................................127-128

KEEPING THE COAT BUTTONED ......................................................................... 128

OUTER JACKETS, COATS, AND SCARVES.............................................................. 129

CHECKING THE COAT...................................................................................... 130

CAPS, HATS, AND TIES ................................................................................... 131

BAD HAIR DAY.............................................................................................. 131

TUCKING IN THE TIE ...................................................................................... 131

SHOES ....................................................................................................... 132

### CORRESPONDENCE

THANK YOU NOTES ........................................................................................ 133

STATIONERY ................................................................................................. 133

### DEFINITIONS

NO HOST AND HOST BAR.................................................................................. 134

FAUX PAS ................................................................................................... 134

RSVP........................................................................................................ 134

SOUP DE JOUR .............................................................................................. 134

FILET AND FILLET........................................................................................... 135

### ENTERTAINING

GUESTS WITH DISABILITIES ........................................................................135-136

PAYING THE BILL.....................................................................................136-137

## FOOD

FOOD TO FACE ............................................................ 137

SOUP AND SHERRY....................................................... 138

BREAD, SOPPING ........................................................ 138

BREAD, HOLDER FOR SOUP............................................ 139

SHARING WITH OTHERS................................................ 139

TOOTHPICKS .............................................................. 140

CHEWING ICE ............................................................ 140

SALT AND PEPPER SHAKERS .......................................... 140

## HOLIDAYS

GIFT GIVING .............................................................. 141

COMPANY PARTIES ...................................................... 142

HOLIDAY CARDS.......................................................... 142

## INTERVIEWING

BASIC MANNERS .......................................................... 143

OVERCOMING NERVOUSNESS .......................................... 144

DRESS AND SUMMER CLOTHING ................................ 144–145

## MEETINGS

OFF SITE.................................................................... 145

ATTIRE FOR COMPANY PICNIC ................................... 145–146

## MISCELLANEOUS

FIRST IMPRESSIONS ...................................................... 146

SPIT AND POLISH ........................................................ 147

SUNGLASSES .............................................................. 147

SMOKING ............................................................ 147–148

OUTSIDE THE OFFICE ENCOUNTERS ................................ 148

HANDKERCHIEF .......................................................... 149

GETTING INTO A CAR ................................................... 149

SEATING RANK IN THE CAR ............................................ 150

NETWORKING WITH BUSINESS CARDS .......................... 150–151

NETWORKING AND FOOD .............................................. 151

TIPPING, BAD SERVICE .................................................. 152

TIPPING, CALCULATING THE TIP ...................................... 153

TRAVEL, AIRPLANE MANNERS .......................................... 154

BIOGRAPHY................................................................ 155

BOOKS AND VIDEOS ..................................................... 157

## HOW TO GET THE MOST FROM THIS BOOK

*Please Don't Drink from the Finger Bowl!*™ is divided into three basic sections: 1) Business Protocol, 2) Dining Protocol, and 3) FAQs— the most frequently asked questions. The sequence of the three sections has been rearranged in this 2008 printing. As in previous printings, many of the sub-sections remain in numbered or bulleted format rather than in paragraph form to make it easier for the reader to find information. New topics include information on *Thank You Notes* and *Accommodating Guests with Disabilities*.

This book emphasizes formal over casual. If you know how to handle a formal setting, you can easily adapt to the casual situation, but not vice versa. The book is not gender specific other than dress code and specific male- or female-related situations.

Anyone can have good manners because manners are a trainable skill. The rules of etiquette are like the rules of driving; standardized throughout with exceptions in different countries. Once you know, practice, and use the basic rules of etiquette; good manners—like driving—become second nature. Practice really does make perfect.

Read the entire book and mark the areas in which you need to improve. Make a list of the specific actions to practice. For example, dine at fine restaurants on a regular basis: 1) to practice good manners, 2) to become more comfortable in a formal setting, and 3) to practice paying the bill. Attend networking events to meet new people, shake hands, and exchange business cards until you are truly comfortable in many settings.

## WHY PROTOCOL IS IMPORTANT

Protocol helps to create a sense of order and provides the guidelines for dining, entertaining, meetings, and even negotiating. Manners and proper etiquette increases one's knowledge and ability to be at ease in a variety of situations.

# WHY PROTOCOL IS IMPORTANT
# IN BUSINESS

Understanding the true value of protocol in business is one of the most important insights into the business world. Protocol, which actually becomes part of a person's value system, is important because protocol shows courtesy and respect. Some employees receive promotions simply because they know and understand protocol and exhibit better manners than their competitors.

In business, the relationship is often noted as an important element to a company's success. Whether in partnerships or alliances or in vendor and client relations, one must be focused on the customer and the issues at hand rather than be worried about which fork to use, which napkin to use, or when to start eating. If you use proper manners, you will help your customer or client feel at ease, comfortable, and most importantly—truly special.

People are more comfortable when they know what to expect and what to do. When people do not know proper protocol, they often appear frozen, even if just for a few moments. One can tell within seconds at a formal dinner who knows what to do and who doesn't.

Know you are being observed. Many savvy leaders watch others the moment they appear. Be on your best behavior from the moment you arrive in the parking lot until you leave (from the parking lot).

Bad manners can adversely affect one's career. A candidate may not be hired because he or she exhibited poor manners during the interviewing process. An employee may not receive a promotion because he or she lacks good manners. Just know that rarely is anyone told that his or her poor behavior or lack of manners was the deciding factor he or she was passed over.

At many protocol seminars, people will come up afterwards to share their story and tell me how they wish they had not underestimated how important protocol was to reaching their career goals. By the time they figured it out, it was too late for their career. Don't wait to learn proper protocol.

Because business casual dress has lowered the professional image of many companies, professional dress and business manners have become more valued. Companies, looking for ways to diversify, are upgrading the company dress code and are expecting better manners of their employees, especially those with direct contact with the customer.

## WHY PLEASE DON'T DRINK
### from the FINGER BOWL!

*Please Don't Drink from the Finger Bowl!* was written because of numerous requests from clients to expand the information in my first book, *Manners for Success®*. The title *Please Don't Drink from the Finger Bowl!* was selected as a lighter approach to a serious subject.

Why the finger bowl? The finger bowl, used more at formal events, is actually a small, clear bowl filled with warm water and placed on an under-plate for each diner. The finger bowl is presented after a finger food course for the purpose of cleansing one's fingers. The water in the finger bowl should not be mistaken as a clear soup, which actually happens more than one would expect.

Although not verified, a story is told about Queen Victoria and a guest who promptly "drank" his finger bowl during a formal meal. The shorter version of the story relates that while the other guests were aghast, the Queen simply picked up her finger bowl and also drank the liquid. The rest of her guests followed suit. The message of her actions was to *never embarrass a guest*, thus, fulfilling the role of the gracious and respectful hostess.

# Section I: Business Protocol

# A. NETWORKING

*"Networking is the most basic level—the starting point—of building relationships. Reach out to others; you never know when you'll meet a valued mentor or a new best friend."*

# NETWORKING

Networking is the first section of this book because relationships are the basis of any business. A successful networking strategy is to build and develop your personal and professional web of contacts for mutually beneficial long-term relationships. Networking creates the opportunity to connect with others in a business or social environment. Networking is much more than just meeting and greeting, shaking hands, and exchanging business cards.

Networking events can be time- and cost-efficient for building business. Networking is also a form of direct sales and face-to-face cold calling for prospective customers. At networking trade shows, one may be given the opportunity to introduce products and services to prospects as well as to existing customers.

Organizations value employees who have strong social skills and are comfortable in many situations. You may sense that you are on exhibit when you attend company and networking events. Guess what? You are. One of the reasons to know and practice good networking skills is to reduce business and social anxieties.

From successful people to new hires, many people are uncomfortable at large gatherings when they do not know a lot of people—or even if they do. A large or small group of strangers can intimidate even the extroverted and experienced. At company gatherings or meetings, the change in circumstance can throw people off their normal confidence level.

Learn to benefit from, not dread company events. The key is to *look and feel like you belong*. Looking like you belong will make you appear and feel more comfortable. Know you are not alone if you feel awkward or nervous. The more you attend networking events, the better you will get, but only if you try to improve. Observe those who are skilled at networking. Critique yourself after each event and focus on improving specific skills before the next event. Without specific purpose, there can be no specific improvement.

# NETWORKING GUIDELINES

1. MOTIVATION

2. NETWORKING STRATEGY

3. THE CAREER or BUSINESS CARD

4. NETWORKING SYSTEM

5. OVERCOMING SHYNESS

6. NETWORKING SKILLS


# 1. MOTIVATION

**Why Are You Really There?** Many attend networking events because they are required by their job (or position) to promote public relations and to show goodwill. Some attend to meet new clients and visit with existing ones, while others attend without any specific business goals—they are there more for social reasons.

Regardless of the motivation, you should know the real purpose of why you are attending and what you want to accomplish at the event. Otherwise, you are just showing up and are *just in the room*.

**How Do You Really Feel About Going To The Event?** Successful networking is not for the lazy or weak. Sometimes one may feel too tired or physically unable to go. Some may have had a difficult day mentally and just cannot seem to think straight. Others simply cannot stand the thought of going to yet another event.

If you are feeling mentally or emotionally negative about attending, get over it before you go to the event. Negativity shows.

Learn to push yourself because that is what it takes. It takes energy and effort—and action—to get results.

**Why Is It Important To Be At Your Best?** First impressions can become lasting impressions. Remember, what you do and say, as well as how you act at any event can be remembered for a long time—perhaps longer than you wish. Your behavior should make a positive impression rather than a lasting negative imprint.

First impressions happen faster than you might think. In fact, first impressions, which are based on your total professional appearance and behavior, can be made in three to seven seconds!

People are attracted to those with power, title, fame, and especially to those who appear relaxed and comfortable at the event. Quality referrals as well as new friends may come from networking; you might even meet your new best friend. One seminar attendee called to share that the person seated next to him at one of my University protocol seminars actually did become a new best friend.

**Be Proactive Rather Than Reactive:** Have a networking plan and be prepared. Do your homework. Have a system and strategy before you go. Don't wait for others to find you; reach out and meet those you want to know.

**Practice:** Attend every networking event you can if for no other reason than to practice social skills. The more you attend the more comfortable and skilled you will become. Get *out of yourself* and focus on others. As you make more friends and establish more business connections, you will begin to truly enjoy networking.

**Expect Success!** Scientists tell us that the brain cannot tell the difference between fantasy and reality. Never think that you are not good at meeting others. Set your own mental expectations. Tell yourself before you go to this event that you will enjoy the event and that you will be successful at networking.

## 2. NETWORKING STRATEGY

**People Goals:** Have specific networking goals and objectives. How many people will you greet and how many will you meet? Which organizations or companies do you want to meet?

**Information Exchange:** What do you want them to know *about you*? Prepare a short introduction about yourself. Avoid giving out brochures unless you are exhibiting in a booth at the event. What specific information do you want to know *about them*? Know which questions to ask to get the information you want to know.

**Networking Tools:** Which tools are appropriate for your goals? Do you have professional appearing business cards, a business card case, and a permanent name badge that is easily read by others?

**Behavior:** Think about how you will behave *before* you get there. Will you treat this as a serious business opportunity or more of a social event?

## 3. THE CAREER or BUSINESS CARD

The career card (for those seeking employment) or the business card (for those who are employed) is an important part of how you communicate your current status. The career or business card represents you when you are not there. Either card: 1) provides contact information, 2) shows the image you choose to portray, 3) is your silent representative, and 4) is a reminder of your meeting.

### General Guidelines: Creating the Career or Business Card
- Your business or career card should portray your desired image. Pay attention to font style and size, the logo, and the graphics.

- Professionally printed cards generally look more professional than computer-printed cards. However, a computer-printed card is better than no card, especially if you're in transition.

- Invest in the highest quality card you can afford. Remember, the thicker the card, the more successful you *appear.*

- If you are just getting started and your contact information will be changing, order or print only a small quantity of cards.

- You do not have to put every contact digit on the card. Place primary digits on the front side and secondary digits (e.g., fax number, secondary cell phone) if important, on the back side.

- Do not fill up the front side of the card with too large a font or too much information. Leave some blank space to enhance the visual appearance and to provide space for notes.

- Make sure the font *style* is easily read and the font *size* is large enough to be read from a reasonable distance.

- Use the back of the card to print a motto, mission statement, quote, or less-important digits.

## 4. NETWORKING SYSTEM

**What Time Will You Arrive?** Arrive early—but not too early—to avoid imposing on those setting up for the event. If you arrive too early, wait to go in or return at the appointed time.

**Guidelines for Arriving:** Arrive within the middle half (of the total time) of the networking event. For cocktail parties, arrive within the first 10-15 minutes. For dinner or luncheon events, arrive a few minutes early or on time. For business events, arrive 15 minutes early or close to on time. If you are late, apologize.

**Before You Go to the Event**
- Know the dress code and plan what you will wear to the event well in advance. If the dress code is not stated, ask the planner or host organization.

- Be appropriately dressed for the event. When in doubt, dress conservatively. Remember, it is better to be overdressed in traditional dress than to be too casual.

- Make sure you are current on the day's latest news. Read newspapers, watch the television news, and check out the latest magazines, or scan the Internet. Be knowledgeable about what is happening on that day in your city, state, and in the world.

- Review industry newsletters and trade journals before attending an industry conference. Be the person in the know.

- Go prepared. Do not wait until you get to the event to think of something to say, especially if you are shy. Have several appropriate stories of interest that you are able to share.

- Avoid long, complicated stories. Keep stories short and easy (for you) to tell. Practice your stories and your approach.

- Have a sufficient supply of business or career cards ready, available, and accessible. Keep extra cards in your car or satchel.

- Prepare a *30-second commercial,* which is a tagline for introducing yourself. Regardless of the actual length, be prepared to tell something about yourself and your organization in less than a minute. Be prepared to elaborate if someone asks you for more information. Write and practice your introduction until you are totally comfortable with saying it.

## How to Work a Crowd

- Check out the crowd when you first enter. What is the mood of the crowd? Get a feel for the energy of the room and the positioning of groups and cliques.

- One of the best places to start is at the beverage or food station(s) because people usually gathered around these areas.

- At each event, try to meet at least three new people you would like to know, whether for personal or professional reasons.

- For an easy entry, start visiting with an acquaintance first and move graciously on soon after. How to move on graciously? Just say, "I've really enjoyed meeting/talking with you," or "It was great to visit with you," and then go to another person.

- How long to visit with each person? In some situations, only a few moments, while in other situations one should stay long enough to learn something of value about the other person.

- To truly work the crowd, move about the entire room. Do not stay with just your friends or with the same group the entire event. Unless you are with your boss and the boss wants you to stay close, move from group to group or to another person.

- Do not be shy about introducing yourself to a stranger. The more you do it—the easier it will get. If you are shy, remember that many are shy, too, and are feeling the same way you feel.

- Smile, relax and have a good time. People like to approach a pleasant, happy person. It really can be that simple.

## Approaching a Group of Strangers

- Observe the body language of the group before you approach. Avoid a group if it looks like a circled wagon, which is a closed group of two or more in intense conversation.

- Start with a group that appears to be physically opened and engaged in a more casual conversation. When you first approach a group, watch for eye contact. If their eyes do not acknowledge you within a few seconds, move to a new group.

- Do not interrupt. Wait for an appropriate time to: 1) approach a group, 2) introduce yourself, and 3) enter the conversation; don't start talking immediately.

**What to Say**

- Begin a conversation is with, "Hello! My name is…What's your name?" Ask questions about them; ask why they are attending the meeting, or what they think about the day's events.

- People really do like to talk about themselves. Focus on the other person, rather than on yourself. Ask questions about his or her work or interests. Focusing on others: 1) takes the emphasis and focus off of you, 2) helps decrease any anxiety you might have, and 3) helps you relax while the focus is on them.

- Be a great listener. People who listen are considered more intelligent and articulate than the person talking—even though the listener may say little.


## 5. OVERCOMING SHYNESS

Know that many people are truly shy and reserved. The Shyness Research Institute estimates that more than 40 percent of the general population consider themselves to be shy. So, if you are shy, you are not alone. Remember that showing up is not enough. The key is to show up and to actively meet and greet others.

If you are shy and find networking difficult, force yourself to attend networking events. Know that many extroverts can have a moment of anxiety before meeting strangers, too. As painful as it might be at first, it really can get easier.

Keep it simple. Ask questions about those you meet. Be prepared with an easy-to-give introduction of yourself. Be prepared with the day's news or other generic topics of general interest.

Not all successful business people and leaders are extroverts. An extrovert gains energy from being with others, while an introvert gains energy from within. In fact, many of the most successful leaders are reserved and uncomfortable at non-business events.

## 6. NETWORKING SKILLS

**Networking skills include:**
A. The Proper Handshake
B. The Exchange of Career or Business Cards
C. Introductions
D. Remembering Names

### A. The Proper Handshake
The handshake is the most basic act of the greeting and connection.

To shake hands:
- A proper handshake is: firm, web-to-web (between the thumb and index finger), flat palm-to-palm, and two to three *shakes.*

- Always shake hands with a firm, confident grip. Avoid shaking hands so firmly that you cause pain. A weak or incomplete handshake can indicate inexperience or a lack of confidence.

- Make sure your hands are clean and dry. Never shake hands with a cold damp hand. At business social events, hold a cold drink in your left hand so the right hand stays dry and warm.

- Holding a person's hand for too long becomes *hand holding.* Clasping one's hand over the handshake is considered a *hand hug,* so be careful how and when you use this handshake.

- Always offer your handshake to people you meet. If you are seated, stand to greet someone. When greeting, look people in the eye and smile—a smile goes a long way.

- If you offer your hand and the greeter does not respond, simply lower your hand. The old rule that women are supposed to offer their hand first is obsolete in our business culture.

- Remove gloves when shaking hands (in business).

## B. The Exchange of Career and Business Cards

Although the business card exchange is not as formal in this country as in other cultures, the business card is still an important exchange of information in our culture.

- **The Career Card:** If you are not employed and are seeking employment, create a career card. The career card should only contain personal contact information you feel safe to share. You may wish to create and designate an e-mail address specific to your employment search. The quality of the career card should be of the same quality you would want in a business card.

- **The Business Card:** An employee's business card is usually provided by the organization. These cards provide information about the company, the employee, title, address, and direct contact information. The employee rarely has any control on the development and issue of these cards.

- **Quantity:** For networking events, take more career or business cards than you think you will need. Keep a supply at your virtual office or in your car if you travel on business.

- **Accessible:** Make sure you can retrieve your business cards quickly and with ease. When someone takes a long time to locate his or her card or appears nervous, it may indicate he or she does not often deal with others outside his or her office.

- **Business Card Case:** Invest in a classic business card case. Cases come in a variety of styles and prices. The use of a card case is the more professional way to present your card. It also protects the cards from curling and keeps the cards clean.

- **Location:** In addition to a business card case, keep cards in your writing binder or writing pad for easy access at meetings. Keep cards in satchels or purses. Business cards kept in wallets have a tendency to curl at the edges. To prevent this, place the business cards in the dollar-bill section.

- **Condition:** Keep cards clean and wrinkle-free. Never give someone a torn, marred, or dirty business card.

- **The Presentation and Exchange:** Present the card with the front side (right side up) facing the other person. Don't cover the face of the card. If someone asks for your card, it is a nice courtesy to reciprocate and ask for his or her business card. Do not hand out your cards too readily. Wait at least until after a few minutes of conversation to give or ask for a card.

- **Receiving the Card:** Receive a person's business card with respect, grace, and interest. Read the card immediately upon receiving. Don't put the card in your pocket first. Take time to read it carefully and pay attention to the key information.

- **Back of Card:** After reading the front of a card, turn the card over for additional information. Businesses will often put the company's vision or mission statement on the back.

- **No Exchange:** Please know that some may not want you to have his or her card. If someone says he does not have a card, do not push him with multiple requests. The individual will get you the information if he or she really wants you to have it.

- **Card System:** Have an *in and out* system for networking events. Keep your cards (outgoing) in your left pocket and place the incoming cards you receive in your right pocket.

- **Formal Events:** Business cards are rarely exchanged at formal business events. If it is done, it's done quickly and very discretely. Never exchange business cards at the formal table.

- **Writing on a Business Card:** Do not write on someone's card in front of them. Some cultures take offense if you make notes on the face of their business card. A safe policy is to only write notes on the card after you have left the event.

## C. Introductions

Introductions are an important part of networking because the introduction is the personal connection to others.

Rules for Introductions:

- Introduce *to the power.*

- Introduce a lesser rank to a higher rank.
  *"Mr. Not-the-Leader, I'd like to introduce you to Mr. Leader."*

- Introduce younger to older. If the higher-ranked person is younger, introduce by rank rather than age.
  *"Sally Younger, I'd like to introduce you to my mother, Mrs. Older."*

- In a social setting, a man is introduced to a woman, but in business, rank is the determinate.

- **Introduce Everyone in the Group:** Always introduce everyone. Don't omit anyone. When making an introduction, make some descriptive statement (position, job, or hobbies) about the person you are introducing to help people find common ground.

- **State Your Name:** A nice courtesy is to state your name during an introduction even though you think the person already knows your name. If someone mispronounces your name, correct him or her (with kindness) at that time rather than have the person continue to mispronounce your name.

- **Stand for Introductions:** If you are seated, it's proper to stand to meet someone, except: 1) when you are seated in a situation that would be disruptive to others if you stood up, and 2) for women in social settings; they may remain seated.

- **Eye Contact:** Always look the other person directly in the eye. Direct and friendly eye contact is most important in introductions because it shows that you are confident and comfortable.

## D. Remembering Names

A person's first and last names are the most important words to that person. If you are telling yourself that you are not good at names, you will not be. Start now to change your attitude about your ability to remember names. Simply by remembering names, you distinguish yourself in the marketplace. Even more importantly, you will make a powerful impression because people appreciate the person who knows—and says—their correct names.

To increase your ability with names:

- Focus on the person's name and the pronunciation when he or she says it. Look closely at the person when his or her name is said. It is appropriate to ask someone how the name is spelled. Clarify the pronunciation if you did not understand it.

- Request a business card and read his or her name while you are with the person. The combination of audio and visual can help to increase one's memory of the name. Some remember because it's visual while others remember because of the audio.

- Repeat (audio) a person's name several times while you are talking to him (or her) to reinforce memorizing the name. Look at his name badge and business card for a visual reminder.

- If you cannot remember a person's name and you cannot see his name on the name badge, admit you cannot remember. Your body language will give you away if you try to bluff.

    Here are two possible things to say:
    1. *"I'm sorry, what is your name again?"*

    2. *"I apologize. I know I should know your name. Please tell me."*

# Section I: Business Protocol

# B. BUSINESS COMMUNICATIONS

*"The art of verbal and written communication is
necessary for any manager or executive."*

# TELEPHONE MANNERS

## General Telephone Guidelines

- Remember, you *really can hear a smile over the phone*. Always talk with a warm, modulated, and friendly tone of voice.

- For a more professional image, answer the phone with either "hello," "good morning," or "good afternoon."

- Always identify yourself and your company, no matter how well you think the other person remembers you. Do not call someone and say, "It's me," or only give your first name.

- Always return telephone calls promptly—at least within the first three rings.

- If you work with customers and clients over the phone, place a mirror close to your desk so you can see yourself while talking on the phone. When you get upset, your face begins to tense and then your vocal cords will tighten. The mirror lets you know you are becoming tense and alerts you to relax.

- Do not put callers on hold for a lengthy time. Ask if you could call them back—and be sure to do so as soon as you can.

- Provide or request sufficient information while you have the other person on the telephone. Avoid having to call him or her back because you forgot to ask or tell them something.

- Avoid making annoying sounds such as clicking your teeth or your tongue. Avoid mumbling. Speak clearly and distinctly.

- Do not eat while talking on the telephone. Do not chew or smack gum while talking on the phone. Just because gum chewing is on the increase, it doesn't mean it's proper or acceptable in public.

## MAKING TELEPHONE CALLS

- When making a call, plan what you are going to say. Have a list or script of the points you want to cover. Writing a list: 1) helps one to stay focused, 2) serves as a checklist to cover all the points, and 3) prevents lengthy and unproductive chitchat.

- Know the name of the person you are calling, not just his or her title. Always investigate to find the person's name before you talk with him or her. You are expected to know the name.

- Know how to pronounce his or her name. If you do not, clarify the pronunciation at the start of the conversation. Also, ask for the correct spelling of the person's name for your records.

- State your name at the beginning of the call and mention how you met the person, if that's a factor.

- What's the purpose? Be clear and specific *why* you are calling.

- When making calls, respect the other person's time. Ask if this is a convenient time to talk. If he (or she) says he only has a few minutes to talk, believe him and respect his time limit.

- Allow time for a brief transition discussion. Avoid going into your request or sales pitch immediately after you say hello. To build relationships you must get to know the other person. At the same time, do not spend more time on small talk than you do on the business at hand.

- Be courteous and appreciative when ending the conversation. Show gratitude even for minor assistance—a thank you goes a long way.

- Be sure to end the conversation with a clear, "Goodbye." Don't ever let someone think that you hung up on them.

## VOICE MAIL MANNERS

- When leaving a message, state your name and number at the *beginning* rather than the *end* of the message. This helps the listener retrieve your contact information quickly if he or she has to replay the message. People are not always at their desk or in a place where they can write down your message.

- If you have no choice but to leave a lengthy message, give your name and number at the beginning *and* the end of the message.

- Slow down and speak clearly when leaving your name and telephone number. Because it's so familiar to us, we speed up when leaving our own name and telephone number.

- Be concise. Specify the action or information you want or need. If at all possible, do not leave long voice mail messages.

- Avoid telephone tag. Are there other ways to connect? After a few telephone tags, leave your e-mail address on the voice mail for them to e-mail you.

## RECORDINGS

- Keep your voice mail greeting current, businesslike, and brief.

- If you leave a daily recorded greeting, make sure your voice sounds fresh and enthusiastic—every day! Slow down, relax, and take the necessary time to record a clear and understandable message. It's the difference between a good or bad impression.

- Avoid a long, confusing pyramid-voice mail system that takes too much time to listen to. These are annoying and if you're too hard to reach, the caller may never call you back.

# CELL PHONE PROTOCOL

The cell phone, which has revolutionized telephone communications, is increasing our ability to communicate daily, anywhere, and anytime. On the downside, the misuse of cell phones has invaded previously private and respected quiet zones.

- Always turn your cell phone off, change to vibrate, or reduce the volume before attending an event or business meeting. Turn the cell phone off while at a concert, hospital, or a library.

- Do not use a cell phone on an elevator where others can hear your conversation. You're holding them cell phone hostage.

- When talking on your cell phone in public, be considerate of those around you, as well as the person with whom you are talking. Telephone conversations should be private.

- Cell-Yell: Do not disturb others with loud conversation or inappropriate language. The microphone volume on the cell phones is set so no one has to yell to be heard.

- Be careful not to reveal proprietary company information while talking on cell phones in public. You never know where your adversaries or competitors are; they could be around the corner or across the way listening to your every word. It happens.

- Use cell phones at social events only if absolutely necessary. If you have a potential emergency, inform the host that you need to leave your cell phone on; switch to vibrate if possible.

- Do not use your cell phone while driving. If you're in transit, pull your vehicle off the road to a safe area to make any calls.

- Do not read or send text messages during meetings. The meeting leaders or speakers actually can see you working on your cell phone, no matter how well you think you're hidden.

# E-MAIL PROTOCOL

- **Subject Lines:** The best subject line is a concise and clear description of the content of the e-mail. To protect against computer viruses and spam, recipients delete numerous e-mails without ever reading them. If the recipient believes the subject line indicates the content is junk, those e-mail also are deleted before being read. Every subject line should relay pertinent content which the recipient will feel safe to open.

- **Value:** When sending e-mails, think it through—does this e-mail have real value to the recipient(s) or is it more self-serving to you. Recipients are receiving an overload of e-mail messages because e-mails are being used to: inform, update, network, advertise, greet for holidays and birthdays, spam, create correct e-mail addresses, and send e-newsletters.

- **Fonts:** Avoid using difficult-to-read font (unusual or fancy). While the recipient's system may not recognize all fonts, most systems recognize Times New Roman, Arial, or Verdana.

- **Salutations and Signatures:** E-mails have almost replaced the formal business letter. For a more formal e-mail business communication, use a salutation (i.e., "Dear Charles:") and a signature (i.e., "Sincerely yours,") in an e-mail. Whether you use a formal or cutesy script font (avoid cutesy in business) for the signature of your name, be sure it is readable.

- **Contact Information:** Add complete contact information in the signature area of your e-mails. Make it convenient for the recipient to be able to contact you in other ways.

  Include contact information such as your name, title, company name, address, telephone number (land line and cell), fax, and website. Also, include your *eight-digit* zip code (the additional four digits help to speed package delivery time).

- **Company Policies:** Company e-mail systems may neither be private nor confidential. Know and understand the company e-mail and Internet policies; be wise in the e-mails you send via intra-company and in which e-mails you open.

- **Personal E-mails:** Do not send or receive personal e-mails on a company computer or virtual office laptop. Companies have ownership rights for *any information* placed on company-owned computers. Know and understand the company policies.

- **Attachments:** Make sure the recipient is able to receive the attachment(s) you send. Some companies have sensitive firewalls and anti-virus systems to block attachments, so verify he or she received it if you have any doubt the attachment went through.

- **Forwards:** Avoid sending unsolicited *forwards* or non-business messages to business associates—especially the cutesy ones.

- **Mail or E-mail:** To measure the importance of an e-mail message, ask yourself: Would you take the time to make a copy, place it in an envelope, stamp, and send this information? Would you send the information in a company memorandum? If you answered "no" to both questions, think twice before sending the e-mail. Don't waste the recipient's time or yours.

- **Replies:** When replying, begin the e-mail with a reference sentence to connect your reply to his or her request or inquiry. If possible, add the reference to the subject line.

- **Reply to All:** Before replying to everyone on the recipient list, consider if everyone will want to (or should) receive your reply. Reply only to those impacted by your response.

- **Content:** Keep e-mail messages brief and to the point. Avoid overusing the high priority symbol especially when the content is not that important. Avoid using cute icons and smiley faces.

- **Copies and Blind Copies:** Be wise in adding recipients to the *copy* and *blind-copy* list. Some compare blind copies to having someone eavesdrop on your e-mail conversation.

  Blind copies are useful when protecting e-mail addresses of the recipients. Unless you want all the recipients to have the e-mail address of everyone on the recipient list, send the e-mail to yourself and then blind copy everyone else on the send-to list.

- **E-Mail Versus Handwritten Notes:** E-mail thank you messages are not a good substitute for handwritten thank you notes, personal notes, or holiday cards. However, an e-mail note is better than no note at all. Use wisely.

- **E-mail Yell:** E-mail Yell, words written with all capital letters, is considered e-mail shouting. SEE WHAT I MEAN!

- **Computer Spell Check Systems:** Do not rely totally on your computer's spell-check systems. Review and edit all of your e-mails closely before sending. For lengthy e-mails, editing is best done with a printed hard copy.

- **E-mail Addresses:** In business, an e-mail address should reflect a professional persona. Young people entering the job market will appear more serious with a professional appearing e-mail address. Avoid using numbers representing your birthday or age. Avoid using cutesy or trendy words. Some recipients will not open any e-mail that does not have a recognizable e-mail address or name.

- **Deleting E-mails:** Senders mistakenly believe that once they have deleted an e-mail, it is gone forever. Wrong. Most e-mails can be retrieved in a company hard drive. Be wise about what you send. If the e-mail is something you would not want to see on the front page of a major newspaper, then don't send it.

## THANK YOU NOTES AND LETTERS

**General:** Thank you notes are fast becoming a lost art. Develop the habit of writing thank you notes to anyone who has been helpful. Since so few send thank you notes today, your note may be more special to the receiver than you might think. (see page 133)

**Interviewing:** The thank you note is an important element of the interviewing process. When writing that all important *after an interview* thank you note, be sure to restate your interest in the position and company in the thank you note. Write a handwritten note; this is not the time to send an e-mail thank you.

Thank you notes are not just for the hiring person, but also for anyone who has helped you through this process. Perhaps your teacher, advisor, mentor, the person who recommended or referred you, and the human relations contact in the organization may all deserve a handwritten thank you note.

An award-winning teacher told me that in 12 years of writing student recommendations, she had received only one thank you note from a student! You can be sure she remembers that student.

**When to send:** Send as soon as possible. For job interviews, mail the thank you within 24 hours, if possible. Remember, others who interviewed that day may also be writing thank you notes. This is one of those times you want to be first!

## GENERAL GUIDELINES

**Handwritten:** The handwritten note is preferred over a typed thank you because it is more personal than a typed note. Why? Because it's written in your unique personal style as opposed to a standard produced font that lacks the personal touch. When writing a handwritten note, be sure to take to time to write legibly.

**Content:** The thank you note is about them, not you. Limit the number of I's used to start your sentences. When your finish writing the note, count the number of I's you used. Although a few are acceptable, avoid too many. For a thank you of four sentences, no more than one sentence should start with an "I." That's a ratio of 25 percent, which is a reasonable guideline to follow.

When writing a thank you, it's important to be clear as to why you are thanking them. The best thank you notes are not only personal, the note is written with a purpose and in an appropriate manner.

**Salutation:** Be sure to use a salutation such as, "Dear Mr. Kenny." Use Mr. or Ms. as the salutation unless you have received permission (they've directly asked you to call them by their first name) to use their first name. Don't assume that because you have met them in person that you are on a first name basis.

**Signature:** The thank you note should always have an ending signature such as "Sincerely," "Truly," or "Warmest regards."

**Structure:** Avoid too many short sentences. Lengthy sentences can be difficult to decipher. Read your note out loud to verify that it's easy to read. Does your note sound conversational or too stiff?

**Style and Stationery:** Always use classic and traditional note cards for professional situations. Traditional stationery is either ivory or white and of a good quality paper stock. Stationery and card stores stock basic thank you notes. Do not send a pre-printed note; select stationery that is blank on the inside. Use colorful and fun casual stationery for personal notes to friends and family. Do not use casual stationery for business or for interview thank you notes.

**E-mail Thank You Notes:** The e-mail thank you is considered a casual thank you. Try to avoid using e-mails for thank you notes if at all possible. However, if you have no other choice but to send an e-mail thank you, an e-mail is better than no thank you at all.

# Section I: Business Protocol

# C. GENERAL BUSINESS MEETINGS

*"Attendees at business meetings play as important a role as the meeting leaders."*

# GENERAL GUIDELINES

The following are guidelines for business meetings and events, whether on- or off-site.

**RSVP:** RSVP is from the French phrase *repondez s'il vous plait,* which means *please reply.* Please respond within the deadline whether you will attend or not. The RSVP is important to the event planner(s) to determine room and seating arrangements, transportation, the number of meals, and the number of handouts.

**Showing Up:** Always show up. Will you be noticed if you attend? Maybe. If you do not? Absolutely. Be there.

**Be On Time:** Arrive a few minutes early. Better to be early than late. Often key information is explained in the first minutes.

**Business Cards:** Take a sufficient supply of business cards.

**Professional Imprint:** What you do, what you say, and how you act and smell, all add up to your total imprint. It takes only three to seven seconds for others to form an opinion about you. Anytime you are on company time, it is time to be "on."

**Networking:** Meet and greet your colleagues. Company events provide a valuable opportunity to build internal relationships.

**Travel?** Do not miss your bus, plane, or train. It really looks bad.

**Don't Want to Attend?** Remember that many may feel the same way. It's best to get over it and go with a positive attitude. Some events yield incredible new contacts and new friends.

**Be Proactive:** Rather than just showing up, plan your goals. Know what you want to gain from the session *before* you attend to maximize your knowledge and professional growth.

## BEFORE THE EVENT

**Read The Materials:** Read all the pre-meeting materials and information you receive before the meeting.

**Dress Code:** Read the invitation closely for the dress code requirements. If not defined, contact the organizer. When in doubt, it is always better to be dressed traditionally and conservatively. Dress up rather than dress down to risk being too casual.

## DURING THE EVENT

**Cell Phone:** Turn your cell phone off. Do not take cell phone photos during the session without permission of the speaker or organizer. Avoid reading or sending text messages while in session. An attendee should never videotape or audiotape a speaker without getting his or her written permission in advance.

**Gum Chewing:** Do not even think about it! Leave gum at home.

**Last Comic Sitting:** Sharing your brilliant creative and comedic comments to your neighbor during a session may bring you satisfaction, but whispered side comments and jokes are disruptive.

**Questions:** The best questions are relevant, easy to understand, specific, concise, and limited to one question at a time. Avoid asking questions that benefit only you; discuss these questions with the speaker after the session. Don't ask so many questions that you dominate the Q and A session.

**Audience Participation:** Participate, interact and contribute, but avoid trying to dominate the session with your comments. Respect and listen to your colleagues and the leader.

**Listen:** Listening is an art. Give full attention to the speaker and your colleagues during group discussions.

## AFTER THE EVENT

**Thank You:** If you enjoyed the session, at least verbally thank the planners, coordinators, and speakers. In addition, an e-mail thank you is good, but the handwritten note is the best.

**Evaluations:** Great managers are often great because they are able to fairly evaluate (legibly written or verbal) others with specific, but encouraging recommendations. Provide quality comments and suggestions to help the speakers and planners *improve* the program.

## NAME BADGES

At conferences and meetings, the name badges are used not only for identification, the badges may also be the ticket to meals or events. At trade shows, the name badge helps attendees to quickly determine the category of vendors, buyers, sellers, and visitors.

- Wear the name badge to speed the process of introductions.

- Write your name clearly and large enough for others to see.

- *Print* your name rather than writing it in script.

- Wear the name badge on your right side and close to your shoulder for a clear vision of your name while shaking hands.

- If possible, adjust the around-the-neck name badge to a more *readable* position. Tie the cord to raise the badge towards your neck. If a clip is on the badge, clip the badge to your collar on your right side.

- Do not stare at someone's chest to read his or her name badge.

# Section I: Business Protocol

# D. BUSINESS CASUAL DRESS

*"Attire and accessories are a major part of the first impression. The level of casual dress should not drop below the level of one's desired professional image."*

# BUSINESS CASUAL DRESS

Business casual dress is one of the most confusing topics of business culture today. What started as a relaxed mode of dress turned into employees wearing clothing suited for gardening, or for working out at the gym. Business casual does not mean sloppy.

The result of an informal survey and a review of more than 70 articles on business casual is that most companies do not tell employees *what to wear,* but tell employees *what not to wear.* Even some of the most prestigious clubs print lists of what is not acceptable, rather than what is appropriate and desirable.

The following lists include both generic topics of what is and what is not acceptable in business casual for men and women.

If you are working with clients and do not know their business dress code, wear traditional business clothing. You can never go wrong by dressing traditionally. When in doubt, dress up rather than dress down.

**First Impressions:** First impressions are often based on one's attire. Believe it or not, a good first impression created by appropriate clothing and personal and business accessories can help determine if you get the job. The right look shows the interviewer you understand the image and expectations of the hiring company.

When an individual is appropriately dressed, he or she will feel and appear more confident and more comfortable. It is not unusual for people to be hired or promoted simply because their attire reflected good judgment. Never underestimate the power of the first impression.

*Remember, a first impression happens within the first few seconds of meeting—not minutes.*

## BUSINESS CASUAL
## FOR BOTH MEN AND WOMEN

- Companies that create an *acceptable to wear* dress code help to establish a consistent image. Providing a list of what not to wear is helpful, but a list with specific dress code examples will get better results. Employees need to know what's acceptable.

- One safe way to know what to wear is to observe the attire of the successful upper managers and executives in your company and dress accordingly. If you are an upper manager, dress to set the example for the staff, employees, and subordinates.

- Style does not always mean expensive. Read fashion magazines for ideas. Watch celebrities, such as the television news anchors (men and women), for trends and examples of clothing, hairstyles, and makeup. Female network television anchors were among the first professional women to wear pantsuits.

- Pay attention to details. Accessories are as important as clothing in presenting the right impression. Check yourself in the mirror before you arrive at the office, before you attend a meeting, and before you meet with a client or customer.

- Dress like the career position in your company or industry to which you aspire.

- Be well groomed. Have a clean body from head to toe, manicured nails (businesslike length and polish), trimmed hair and facial hair and polished shoes. Be sure to use deodorant or antiperspirant (preferably unscented).

- If you use cologne or perfume, please use in small doses (or not at all). Some believe wearing a fragrance is not businesslike while there are some who simply don't like the smell. Some really are allergic to colognes or perfumes.

## BUSINESS CASUAL FOR MEN

## DO NOT WEAR... ⊘

- Tattered or frayed clothing

- Stained clothing

- Wrinkled clothing

- Sweat shirts, sweat or jogging pants

- Casual or biking shorts

- Hiking boots

- T-shirts with logos (except the company logo)

- Printed slogans (except the company slogan)

- Tank tops

- See-through anything

- Tight or suggestive clothing

- Garish prints

- Camouflage fabric

- Sneakers or sandals

## BUSINESS CASUAL FOR MEN

### DO WEAR...

- Pressed or ironed clothes

- Shirts (long sleeves preferred)

- Polo shirts with collars

- Belt (in good condition)

- Matching colors in belt and shoes

- Loafer styled shoes

- Polished shoes

- Socks, always (matching and color coordinated)

- Long socks with slacks

- Slacks, dress or casual

- Long pants (not jeans)

- Pants with a crease

- Crew or v-neck sweaters over shirts with collars

- Unlined or lined jackets

# BUSINESS CASUAL FOR WOMEN

## DO NOT WEAR... $\bigcirc$

- Tattered or frayed clothing

- Wrinkled clothing

- Stained clothing

- Sweat-shirts, pants, or jogging clothes

- Leggings

- Spandex clothing

- Casual or biking shorts

- Hiking boots, sneakers, or sandals

- Ultra-short skirts

- T-shirts with logos (except the company logo)

- Printed slogans (except the company slogan)

- Tank tops or camisoles

- Cropped tops

- See through or suggestive clothing

## BUSINESS CASUAL FOR WOMEN

### DO WEAR...

- Business appropriate dress

- Pressed or ironed clothes

- Business-length skirts

- Skirts that pass the sitting test

- Business height neckline

- Pant suits

- Matching outfits

- Flats, stacked heels, or loafers

- Unlined or lined jackets

- Hosiery (always appropriate)

- Appropriate length socks

- Non-sports logos

- Jewelry that does not clank or make noise

- Subtle or conservative jewelry

# BUSINESS DRESS AND DRESS CODES

**Dress Code-Company:** Read the company policy for the dress code or acceptable attire. If there is no policy, ask the person who hired you what is expected. Also, observe what the successful managers and executives are wearing, but don't base your dress choice on only one person's attire.

**Dress Code-Events:** Generally the invitation will include the appropriate dress code. If no dress code is noted and you're not sure if it's business attire, call the coordinator of the event to clarify.

**Business Dress:** *Men:* Business dress is typically considered a suit and tie. *Women:* Pant or dress suit or traditional dress for women. A camisole under a blazer or other business top is not appropriate, especially if the lace neckline is visible.

**Business Dress for Formal Events:** Galas and fundraisers or other community events may require formal dress. Annual company events may also require formal attire. For company functions, remember you are representing your company and your attire should portray a professional appearance. For men, the black-tie tuxedo is appropriate and for women, a cocktail dress (shorter length than a gown) or a formal gown is appropriate.

Women should avoid dresses or gowns that are too suggestive. Avoid tops that are too low or skirts that are too high for business or company sponsored events.

Men may wear a black suit if the dress code states *black tie optional*. Because the tuxedo is such a successful, distinctive look, men should wear a tuxedo to the proper event whenever possible.

For those who are not used to wearing formal attire, wear the formal attire at home before the event. Get accustomed to the outfit so you don't appear stiff or uncomfortable at the event.

# Section II: Dining Protocol

# A. THE TABLE

*"The distinctive table yields a distinctive memory. The table setting sets the mood for the entire event."*

# TABLE SETTINGS

The *table setting* includes the place settings, all of the linens, table decorations, and condiments. The table setting indicates the level of formality, coveys the theme, and creates the mood for the event.

# TABLE DECORATIONS

Table decorations are the finishing touch to any table setting. The table decorations are part of the attention to detail that guarantees a successful event.

When entertaining for business, even at a fine restaurant, be sure to pay attention to the details of your selected table setting. Table decorations are great conversation starters, especially when the decorations are unusual, creative, or beautifully arranged.

**Floral Arrangements:** The flower arrangement on the table should not block the guests from seeing each other across the table. The arrangement must either be low or high enough to permit a clear view of the guests sitting across the table.

Once you decide how high or low you want your arrangement to be, sit in one of the chairs (one that will actually be used at the event) at the table and measure the viewing space. Because chair and table height vary, make sure the height measurement is correct.

Upon receiving fresh flowers, double check that the flowers are fresh and in water. Flowers delivered early may wilt by the end of a hot day. You never know how long the florist has had the flowers in *or out* of the cooler, so be sure to ask for the freshest flowers.

Be careful not to have too fragrant a flower. You do not want the aroma of the flowers to overwhelm the guests or cause allergic reactions. Consult with your florist about the wisest selection.

Effective floral decorations can be a single flower or a cluster of greenery at each place setting rather than a large center bouquet. A bouquet of fresh mixed greenery is cost effective as well as unusual.

**Fruit Arrangements:** Fresh or dried fruit can also make an interesting arrangement. A container of artichokes, pomegranates, a bowl of nuts (in the shell), a bowl of lemons and limes, or other in-season fruit is a simple, but effective arrangement.

## LIGHTING

**Candles:** Candles can help set the mood of an event. Lit candles also can set a fire if left alone. Candle rules are: 1) light the candles before the first guests arrive, and 2) do not blow the candles out until the last guest departs.

Keep your eye on the candle(s) that might burn too fast or are in line of an air vent. If the candles are burning too fast, you may want to move or extinguish them. Also, watch for dripping candle wax that could harm tabletops or linens. Use dripless, unscented candles.

**Chandeliers:** Chandeliers add to the ambiance of any room or dining event. When using a dimmer switch (controls the intensity and brightness of the chandelier candle lights), do not dim so low that the diners are not able to see what they are eating. Too high a setting gives too bright a light and yields an unattractive glare. Test the desired level of lighting in advance.

## EVENT FAVORS

**Favors:** Favors (and the packaging) must be appropriate to the occasion. Place favors at a spot at each place setting where the favor will not interfere with the place setting and food service.

# TABLE TRASH

Table trash is the term I use for all those wrappers for sugar substitute, sugar, butter, crackers and breadsticks. The table trash can stack up even in formal settings. The best servers/waiters will remove the table trash frequently throughout the meal. The goal is to keep the table as tidy and neat as possible.

**Sugar Packets:** Fold the empty sugar packets and place under the bread and butter plate, which typically remains on the table until dessert. When the server/waiter clears the table for dessert, he or she will remove the empty packets. If there is no bread and butter plate, place the wrapper under the rim of the dinner or salad plate.

During the dessert and coffee course, leave the emptied sugar packets under the rim of the saucer of the coffee cup. If there is no saucer or plate, fold neatly and leave on the table.

**Cracker Wrappers:** It may be difficult to place cracker wrappers under a plate. Since crackers are generally served during a casual salad course, leave these wrappers on the bread and butter plate, to the left side of the plate, or on the salad plate *when you are finished* eating the salad course. Wrapped crackers are usually not served at a formal setting. Serve rolls or breadsticks (unwrapped).

**Butter Wrappers:** Scrape the butter off the wrapper with your knife and place on your bread and butter plate. Because butter wrappers are messy, avoid placing these under a plate or on top of the table. Fold and place on the bread and butter plate.

**Bread Stick Wrappers:** Some commercial bread sticks have a paper wrapping. Simply remove and fold the wrapper and leave under or on the bread-and-butter plate.

# Section II: Dining Protocol

# B. PLACE SETTINGS & CONDIMENTS

*"Attention to details of the proper place setting
is noticed and greatly appreciated by the guests."*

# THE PLACE SETTING

A *place setting* consists of the dinnerware, stemware, and flatware, and individual condiments for each person at the dining table.

Etiquette requires that one knows:
1) Which components of the place setting are his or hers.
2) The purpose of each piece.
3) The proper way to use the forks, knives, spoons, and serving pieces to avoid making a faux pas at the dining table.

One wrong choice to the right or left can throw the entire table off. A guest should drink from his appointed stemware and should use his appointed bread and butter plate for his bread. Too often, guests do not know which components belong to them and their immediate discomfort is apparent through their body language.

**Dinnerware:** A basic five-piece place setting includes a dinner plate, salad plate, bread and butter plate, and cup and saucer. Plates for additional courses may be added. For example, the White House has sufficient components to set at least a 20-piece place setting for a State Dinner for numerous courses.

**Flatware:** A basic four-piece place setting consists of a knife, fork, salad/dessert fork, and teaspoon. Basic flatware will vary in size.

When a meal is served in multiple courses, the flatware for some courses may be added when each course is served. This reduces the space needed for the flatware required for each setting.

**Stemware:** A basic two-piece place setting of stemware may be either a water goblet and a wine glass, or a water goblet and an iced tea glass. A third stem for wine service may be an additional wine, liqueur glass, or a champagne glass.

# DINNERWARE

## BASIC DINNERWARE PIECES

1. **Dinner Plate★** (10")
   The dinner plate is placed in the center of each place setting one inch from the table edge.

2. **Salad/Dessert Plate** (8")
   The salad plate is placed either to the left of the dinner plate or in the center on top of the service plate. The salad plate may also be used as a dessert plate that is usually placed in the center of the place setting (after the dinner plate has been removed).

3. **Bread and Butter** (6")
   The bread and butter plate is placed on the left side of the dinner plate just above the forks.

4. **Cup and Saucer**
   The cup and saucer are placed to the right of the dinner plate or the spoons. Cup handles are aligned on the outer right side.

5. **Rim Soup Plate, Soup Bowl or Cup**
   Soup plates (rim), soup cups and bowls are usually placed on an under-plate, which is a saucer or plate (flat) wider than the soup plate or bowl. The soup service may also be served on top of the charger plate. A non-entrée soup is generally served and removed before the dinner plate is placed on the table.

6. **Service Plate or Charger★** (12")
   The service plate, also called a charger plate, is used as a buffet plate or as a service plate in a formal event. Service plates may also be used as under-plates for the appetizer, soup or salad.

   *★Note: Sizes are approximate and will vary by pattern.*

# BASIC DINNERWARE SETTING

Bread and Butter Plate

Salad Plate        Dinner Plate        Cup and Saucer

Service Plate under a Rim Soup Plate (with soup spoon)

# FLATWARE

Flatware is placed per place setting in *the order it will be used—from the outside in. Outside* refers to the outer area of the dinner plate and *in* is towards the center. The flatware used will vary depending on the available flatware implements and the number and type of food courses.

Knives and spoons are placed to the right of the dinner plate and forks on the left side. One way to remember this is to *compare the number of letters on the side of the dinner plate to the number of letters of the flatware.*
For example:
- FOUR letters on the LEFT side = Fork
- FIVE letters on the RIGHT side = Knife, spoon

The dessert flatware, generally the dessert fork (or dessert spoon) and the beverage teaspoon, is placed above the dinner plate. A good way to remember this dessert placement is to make a full circle with your arms in front of you with fingertips touching. If you eat too many desserts you will be this size. The dessert flatware is placed at the touching "fingertips" position at the top of the dinner plate.

## Which Side of the Dinner Plate?
**Left** (a four-letter word) side of the dinner plate
Match with the four-letter words:
- Fork
- Food other than the entrée

**Right** (a five-letter word) side of the dinner plate
Match with the five-letter words:
- Drink    All beverages are on the right
- Spoon    Spoons are on the right
- Knife    The entrée knives are on the right

# FLATWARE

| ITEM | USED FOR |
|------|----------|
| A. | Luncheon fork | Entrée |
| B. | Salad/dessert fork | Salad or dessert |
| C. | Cocktail fork | Seafood |
| D. | Luncheon knife | Entrée or bread |
| E. | Steak knife | Thick meat |
| F. | Fish knife | Fish only |
| G. | Teaspoon | Multiple uses |
| H. | Soup spoon, cream | Thick soup |
| I. | Soup spoon, bouillon | Clear soup |
| J. | Iced tea/parfait spoon | Deep or tall stemware |
| K. | Grapefruit spoon | Grapefruit segments |
| L. | Butter spreader | Individual spreader |
| M. | Ice cream fork | Firm ice cream |

The above items are the most basic flatware pieces in a place setting. The person who knows the basic flatware components can tell which food courses are being served just by looking at his or her place setting. The less a person has to worry about which fork, knife or spoon to use, the more he or she is able to concentrate on the event, his or her table companions and the conversation.

# BASIC FLATWARE PLACE SETTING

## Left Side of the Dinner Plate
- Luncheon–size or dinner–size★ fork
- Salad fork used for salads (non–entrée salads)
- Cocktail fork★★

## Right Side of the Dinner Plate
- Luncheon–size or dinner–size★ knife
  (The knife *blade* faces towards the dinner plate.)
- Steak knife (serrated)
- Fish knife
- Teaspoon, multipurpose
- Soup spoon
- Iced tea spoon
- Grapefruit spoon

## Above the Dinner Plate
- Teaspoon used for coffee or hot tea
- Dessert fork or ice cream fork used for dessert
                   or
- Teaspoon used for coffee or hot tea
- Teaspoon used for dessert

## On the Bread and Butter Plate
- Individual butter spreader. Place either on the top or the right side of the bread–and–butter plate with the edge of the spreader towards the center of the bread and butter plate.

*★The dinner size fork and knife are larger than the luncheon size and are used only at dinners.*

*★★The cocktail fork is not limited to placement on the left side.*

# THE PLACEMENT OF FLATWARE

Remember that flatware is arranged from the outside in; arranged in the order it is used per course. For example, if the first course is a salad, the salad fork is the farthest fork on the left side of the dinner plate. If the second course is a soup, the soup spoon is the farthest spoon on the right side of the dinner plate.

For a multi-course meal, the dinnerware and flatware for each course may be brought to the table for that course and then removed after that course is completed.

## Flatware Placement and Use:

- A luncheon fork or a dinner fork (rather than a salad fork) is used to eat an entrée salad. An entrée salad serves as the main course, such as a Cobb salad or a Chicken Caesar salad.

- The *individual butter spreader* is placed on the bread and butter plate with the cutting edge facing the center of the bread and butter plate.

- The *butter knife*, which looks like a small saber, stays with the main butter dish. The *individual butter spreader,* which is used for spreading, is kept on the bread and butter plate.

- A fish fork and fish knife are used with the fish course. The seafood cocktail fork is the exception to the rule and may be placed in several locations: on the right side, on the left side, or on the seafood cocktail plate.

- A steak knife, placed on the right of the dinner plate, may be served with steak or other thick pieces of meat.

# BASIC STEMWARE

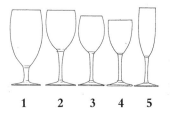

**1    2    3    4    5**

1.  **Iced Tea Glass**
    Place below the water goblet on the right side. The iced tea glass has the largest bowl of all the stems.

2.  **Water Goblet**
    Place at the top of the knife. Always serve water in a water goblet at any formal meal.

3.  **Red Wine**
    Place the red wine stem at the lower right side of the water goblet. The bowl of the red wine stem is larger than the bowl of the white wine. The top of the red wine bowl may be curved inward to hold the bouquet (fragrance) of the wine.

4.  **White Wine**
    Place at the lower right of the red wine glass. The bowl of the white wine stem is smaller than the red wine bowl to help hold the cooler temperature of the white wine.

5.  **Champagne**
    Place in the order of the course. The flute shape stem is the most popular today because it more effectively captures the champagne bubbles and helps retain the cooler temperature.

*Not Pictured: The dessert-champagne stem may be used for champagne or as a dessert dish for ice cream or puddings.*

## STEMWARE ARRANGEMENT

Wineglasses are placed at an angle in the order of use.

Water Goblet    Champagne
White Wine
Red Wine

## HOW TO HOLD STEMWARE

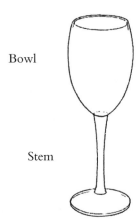

Bowl

Stem

Hold wine glasses by the stem rather than the bowl
to avoid warming the beverage.

## NAPKINS

Napkins are placed: 1) to the left of the forks, 2) on the empty dinner plate, or 3) in a stemware or the coffee cup or teacup. Place your napkin in your lap when you are seated or immediately after the host is seated and has placed the napkin on his or her lap.

Do not completely unfold a large dinner napkin. Unfold so the napkin is folded in half before placing across your lap. In some restaurants the waiter will place the napkin on the lap of women *and* men. This is normal procedure in many upscale restaurants.

## GENERAL GUIDELINES

• If you are leaving the table temporarily and will return, leave the napkin slightly folded on the seat of your chair.

• When you are finished eating your meal, slightly fold the napkin and place to the right of the place setting. Do not place on the dinner plate or any plate containing food.

• NEVER sneeze into your napkin. Excuse yourself and leave the table to a private area to sneeze. Avoid comments about sneezing when you return. If there is nothing available, and one must use the napkin, just know that it leaves a bad impression on more than the napkin. Always have a handkerchief or tissues to prevent the need to use the napkin other than its proper use.

• Use your napkin to dab or gently wipe your mouth. Do not wipe your face with your napkin. Do not dip the tip of your napkin into the water glass to wipe or wash your face.

• When dining during a business meeting, leave your napkin on your lap until the meeting is completed. Otherwise, the table is covered with dirty napkins during the meeting. Another alternative is to ask the waiter to completely clear the table before you conduct your business.

# CONDIMENTS

- Condiments include: salt and pepper, cream, sugar, relishes, au juice sauces, gravy, ketchup, mustards, hot sauce, salsa, chutneys, steak and barbeque sauces, butters, jams and jellies.

- Always taste your food first before adding salt, pepper, or other spices. Otherwise, you may add too much seasoning. Some chefs and cooks believe they have perfectly seasoned the food and may actually be offended if you season your food.

- Tap the tops of the salt shaker and the pepper shaker gently with your index finger to season your food. Do not shake the shakers even though they are called the salt and pepper shakers.

- Salt cellars and pepper cellars are small individual containers that may be used at a formal meal. Use the small spoons in the cellars to lightly sprinkle the salt or pepper over your food.

- Special spreads or sauces can add a lot of flavor to any dish. If you are not sure you will like a sauce, place a small portion on your plate and taste it first.

- Any condiment that requires spreading with your knife is placed on your plate, not directly on the food. Spread the condiment on your food with your knife.

- Place gravy or salad dressing directly on the food. Be careful not to not drench your food with sauce or gravy.

- Do not ask for a condiment if it is not offered. The hostess might consider the request for steak sauce (or other condiment) an insult to the taste of her steak. Another reason is that if the host has forgotten to purchase a condiment, it would be embarrassing to the host if the host cannot satisfy your request.

# PASSING THE FOOD AND CONDIMENTS

- Always pass the salt and pepper together (as a set) even if someone asks you to pass only the salt or the pepper. Consider the salt and pepper a couple who are always together. By passing together, this prevents having to locate one or the other at the opposite end of the table for the guest who wants both.

- Pass the creamer and sugar together around the table. After you have used the creamer, hold by the body of the creamer and turn it so you pass it *with the handle facing* the person receiving the creamer.

- If you want a serving of the food or the condiment while it's being passed, serve yourself first before passing. Otherwise, you have to ask for the food item to be passed right back to you.

- The beverages, bread or rolls, butter, jams and jellies should always be passed around the entire table. The gracious host will watch to see if these condiments need to be passed again.

- Although the guest of honor is always served first, the rules of passing are inconsistent. In fact, many etiquette books do not state one direction to pass, but say use common sense and pass in a convenient manner around the table.

- While some say to pass counter-clockwise (because the guest of honor is seated to the right of the host), the reason the passing rule is not clearly defined is that passing may be dictated by who is being served and who is doing the passing.

- If the table is passing in only one direction, and someone from the opposite direction asks for the item that is close to you, use common sense and pass it to the closest and most convenient direction to that person.

# Section II: Dining Protocol


# C. DINING STYLE & SERVICE


*"Whether formal or casual, treat each course special, just as you would the chapters of a book or the acts of a play."*

## AMERICAN STYLE

In the American style of eating, the *fork is held with the right* hand to eat. The *knife is held in the left hand* to cut food or in the right hand to spread butter, jam, or other spreads.

**How to Hold Flatware:** The stem of the fork is held between the index finger and the third finger (right hand) with the thumb on top of the stem. When cutting foods, the fork is held in your right hand and the knife in your left hand in the American style.

**How to Cut Food:** To cut food with a fork and knife, hold the food with the fork tines facing down in your left hand. Cut the food with the knife. Do not grasp the knife or fork with a clenched fist as if stabbing. After cutting, place the knife (blade facing in) on the edge of the plate and change the fork to your right hand to eat.

**Where to Place the Fork and Knife:** When resting, place the knife (blade facing towards you) on the edge of the plate and the fork on the opposite side of the plate per the diagram below.

**The Finished Position:** When finished, place the knife blade tip (blade facing towards you) pointing at hour 11 on a clock and the bottom of the knife handle at hour 5 on a clock. Place the fork beside and below the knife with the fork tines up. The position appears to be at 5 o'clock as in the end of the workday—the end of the appetizer, salad, or entree course.

American Style
Resting Position

American Style
Finished Position

# CONTINENTAL STYLE

In the Continental or European style of eating, the *fork is held with the left hand* for eating. The Continental system is easier to use because the forks, which are placed on the left side of the dinner plate, are in position for the left hand, and the knives, which are placed on the right side of the dinner plate, are in position for the right hand. There is no switching between hands in this method.

Either the American or Continental style of eating is appropriate in our culture. The continental style is gaining in popularity today.

**How to Hold Flatware:** Hold the fork (tines facing down) with the left hand and the knife with the right hand.

**How to Cut Food:** Cutting food is similar to the American Style and guidelines except the fork is held by your left hand only.

**Where to Place the Fork and Knife:** When resting, the knife (blade facing towards you) is at an angle on the plate and the fork across the knife per the diagram below.

**The Finished Position:** When you are finished, the fork and knife are placed in the 5 o'clock position as in the American style, but with the fork tines down. The position appears to be at 5 o'clock—the end of the work day—the end of the appetizer, salad, or entrée course.

Continental Style
Resting Position

Continental Style
Finished Position

# THE COURSES

The following are examples of the combination of courses:

## Three-course Meal

First Course:     Salad, soup, or appetizer
Second Course:    Entrée
Third Course:     Dessert

## Four-course Meal

First Course:     Appetizer
Second Course:    Soup or Salad
Third Course:     Entrée
Fourth Course:    Dessert

## Six-course Meal

First Course:     Appetizer
Second Course:    Soup
Third Course:     Salad
Fourth Course:    Sorbet
Fifth Course:     Entrée
Sixth Course:     Dessert

## Eight-course Meal

First Course:     Appetizer
Second Course:    Soup
Third Course:     Fish
Fourth Course:    Sorbet
Fifth Course:     Entrée
Sixth Course:     Salad
Seventh Course:   Cheese and Fruit
Eighth Course:    Dessert

*Note: Salads may be served before or after an entrée in a multiple course meal.*

# THE COURSES

**The Appetizer Course:** The appetizer is a starter or first course. Examples of appetizers are shrimp cocktail, raw oysters, Oysters Rockefeller, a stuffed artichoke, or even a small pasta dish.

**The Soup Course:** The soup course is the first, second, third, or entrée course. Soups are either cream or bouillon (clear) based.

**The Salad Course:** Non-entrée salads are generally mixed lettuce greens and/or vegetables served with a dressing, or a fruit mixture.

**Sorbet:** Sorbet, a citrus sherbet or other ice, is served following a highly flavored course to cleanse the palate. Sorbet is not a dessert.

**The Fish Course:** The fish course may be a small to medium-size serving of fish served before the entrée. A larger portion of fish may be served as the entrée. A fish fork and fish knife is usually provided. The fish service is removed before the entrée course.

**The Entrée Course:** The entrée, which is the main course, may be an entrée salad, a pasta, fish, fowl, meat, or casserole dish.

**The Dessert Course:** The dessert course may be a sweet dessert, berries, or fruit served with a sauce or dressing. All the non-dessert implements and condiments are removed before the dessert course.

**The Cheese and Fruit Course:** This course, a selection of cheeses (usually served at room temperature) and a variety of fruits, is served after the entrée and before the dessert course.

**Bread:** Bread, which is not usually considered a course, is offered at the beginning of the meal and remains on the table until after the entrée has been served. Bread is removed before the dessert course.

# THE FINGER BOWL

- The finger bowl is a clear glass bowl containing warm water to cleanse one's fingers following a course that requires eating with one's fingers. Finger bowls are used more in formal dining.

- Do not drink the finger bowl water! It is not a clear soup!

- The finger bowl may be accented with citrus accents, mint leaves, or flowers to add to the appearance. Some accents are a lemon, lime or strawberry slice, or other fruit garnish.

- Do not eat the accents or garnishes that have been placed in a finger bowl—not even if the accent is edible.

- A paper doily is usually placed under a finger bowl (between the finger bowl and the service plate or under-plate).

- Dip the fingers of your hand into the bowl and dry with your napkin—one hand at a time. Do this discretely.

- Do not put your *hand* into the finger bowl; the finger bowl is for fingers only. This cleansing ceremony is a gentle one.

- Do not dip the tip of your napkin into your finger bowl.

- Do not *wash* your face at the table with the water from the finger bowl. The container is only for the fingers.

- When finished, move the finger bowl *and the doily* to the left side of the dinner plate. The waiter may ask if you have completed using the finger bowl before he or she removes it.

- When you simply cannot remember what to do, wait for the host or hostess to begin and follow his or her example.

# FIVE WAYS FOOD IS SERVED

1.  **The plates are filled in the kitchen and served by a waiter(s).** The waiter serves food to you from the left and the drinks are served from the right.

2.  **The plates are filled by the hostess or host at the head of the table and then passed.** If the hostess is serving the food while seated, she fills the plate for the person at the end of the right side of the table first. The guests on the right side of the table keep passing the plates down until the right side has been served. The left side is then served. The hostess serves herself last. Once she has taken the first bite, the guests may begin to eat. Some believe the guest should eat upon being served. Unless the food is going to get cold, I believe the guests can wait so everyone can start at the same time.

3.  **The food is passed on serving platters at the table and each guest serves his or herself.** The platters are served around the table. Use the proper serving pieces on the serving platter to serve yourself. Do not use your fork or knife. Take moderate portions. Serve yourself the garnish that may be on each serving and serve yourself the sauce. Leave the serving implements on the platter so the next person can reach them easily. Be careful not to get food on the serving pieces.

4.  **The food is passed on platters or serving pieces by a waiter(s).** Each guest is served with or without the assistance of the waiter. Take or ask the waiter for a moderate portion. If serving yourself, leave the serving implements on the platter in a position so the next person can reach them easily.

5.  **Buffet Service** The buffet service is used in both casual and formal settings (although not often in formal settings). The buffet service is useful for large groups, more casual entertaining, and is also a convenient way for the single host or hostess to entertain.

## GUIDELINES FOR BUFFET SERVICE

- Some buffets are arranged by buffet stations for separate courses, e.g. a salad station, an entrée station, a dessert station. So, before you start the buffet, look around to see the total offerings.

- If there are separate serving stations for each course, each station will have the appropriate-sized plates for that course.

- A buffet is not an open invitation to overfill your plate. Be wise in the amount of food you take. Most buffets are set up for the diners to easily return to refill their plates. I think one appears more dignified with a moderately-filled plate than an overflowing one.

- If this is a business meeting with the buffet station designated for your group only, return to the buffet station for second servings only after everyone has gone through the line.

- For larger events where there are several buffet stations, you may return to the buffet station(s) several times regardless of how many have gone through the line.

- Do not eat or taste directly from the buffet platters or containers.

- Do not take a taste of the soup from the soup ladle in the soup tureen.

- Put the sauces or dips on your plate. Do not dip any food directly into sauces or dips on the buffet.

# Section II: Dining Protocol

# D. THE BEVERAGE

*"The celebration of many events includes beverages of distinction. Be wise in the usage—and most of all—be professional in the consumption and ceremony of beverage."*

# BUSINESS AND BEVERAGE

One of the more serious issues in business etiquette is the consumption of alcoholic beverages while on *and* off the job. While alcohol can add to the enjoyment of a fine meal or party, too much alcohol consumption by the host or guest can ruin the event.

Heavy alcohol consumption brings up several issues, including health, safety, addiction problems, poor judgment, loss of production, and any possible liability of the company. For each of these issues there is a cost to the organization and to those involved.

Alcohol acts as a depressant and affects one's judgment, as well as his or her reaction time and coordination. A person's judgment can be affected within seconds of drinking alcohol.

**Company Policy:** Many companies have a written policy about alcohol consumption while on the job. Know your company's policy regarding the rules, the expectations, and the liabilities.

The transition from the binge-drinking college days to the business world can be dramatic and a huge clash of the cultures. Make no mistake; companies want and expect *all employees* to be in control of their behavior. If you are a recent college graduate, please understand the expectations of employees at business social events.

**Be Wise, Go Slow, and Go Low:** If you choose to drink, know your limit. Drink fewer drinks, dilute your drinks, and learn to sip rather than guzzle. Take longer to drink them. Be wise.

**What is One Drink?** One drink is one 12-ounce bottle of beer or wine cooler, one 1.5-ounce of 80-proof liquor, or 5 ounces of wine. Mixed drinks from the bar often contain more than *one drink*.

**"No, Thank You."** Please know that not everyone can or wants to drink alcohol. Know that you are never required or obligated to drink. Always feel free to turn down an alcoholic beverage.

# WINE

- Generally, red wines are served with red meats, hearty, or spicy foods, while white wine is served with white entrees unless the white entree is hearty. Today, people drink the wine they prefer regardless of the type of food is being served.

- When selecting wine for a meal, match the intensity of the food with the wine. Serve lighter wine with an appetizer, medium wine with salad or soup, and a heavier wine with a medium to heavy entrée. A sweet wine is served with dessert.

- When serving wine with a salad, select a salad dressing with low acidity to avoid the clash of acidity and the wine. Select a dressing made with balsamic, rice wine vinegar or fruit juice rather than one containing regular vinegar. Regular vinegar has a strong acidity level and can impair the taste of the wine.

- Serve red wine at cellar temperature (around 62-65 degrees F) rather than at room temperature, which is usually higher. Serve white wines chilled, but not cold (around 55 degrees F).

- Vintage (library) wines may be decanted to eliminate sediment, while young wines may be decanted to help the wine *breathe*.

- A sommelier (sô-ma-lyā´) is a wine steward in fine restaurants. The sommelier, an expert in wine service and in the wine selection for the facility, is generally tipped 15 to 20 percent of the wine tab. If you are not familiar with wine, don't hesitate to ask the sommelier for assistance in selecting a wine.

- Although natural corks are still being used to seal wine, a growing percentage of vineyards (even fine vineyards) now use synthetic rather than natural cork. Because natural cork can spoil, wines can be ruined if the natural cork becomes moldy, disintegrates, or allows air to seep into the wine (for any reason). Air negatively affects the quality of stored wine.

# WINE TASTING TEST

Once the wine has been selected, the host will taste test the wine to make sure the wine is acceptable to drink. When entertaining at a facility, review the wine list and if possible, make your selections before the event. In some facilities you may be able to test the wine in advance. To finalize your selection, consider purchasing bottles of your top choices to test before making your final choices.

If you do not have a chance to preview the wine list before the event, be sure to enlist the help of an experienced waiter or the sommelier. Some facilities show the wine selection on the website.

The host should select and test the wine to control the price and quality. If you do not drink alcohol or do not feel comfortable in sending back an unacceptable wine, ask someone from your company (not the client) to select and test the wine. Because bad wine can ruin a fine meal, one would not want his or her client to feel responsible for the selection of the wine if the wine is bad.

Although it is generally not appropriate for a guest to offer to select the wine, it can happen. If your guest is a client and they insist on helping select the wine, you have to decide whether to defer to the client request or risk the downside of denying your client. Remember, a bad wine is minor compared to an unhappy client.

One option is to order the wine yourself and have the client participate in the wine-tasting test. Another option is to confer with the client as to which wine to order so that you both select and taste test the wine(s). A third option is to order both your choice and the client's choice.

If you are the taste tester or have been invited to a wine-tasting event, it is better not to wear perfume or cologne or other strong fragrance such as hair spray. Also, avoid lighting scented candles in the same room where fine wines are being served.

## THE WINE TEST

1.  First, the waiter or sommelier will show the host the bottle and the label for the host to verify it is the wine and vintage (year produced) ordered.

2.  The waiter or sommelier will now open that bottle of wine at the table (to ensure the bottle has not been switched).

3.  Next is the cork test. The cork is important because if the seal of the cork is broken or if the cork is bad, the wine may be spoiled. The waiter or sommelier will place the cork on the table by the host or person conducting the taste test.

    Look for (natural cork): A) a solid cork that is not crumbly, B) a clean cork that is void of mold or other signs of deterioration, and C) one end of the cork is moist, but not soaked through. A dry cork may indicate the wine was not stored properly on its side to keep the cork moist.

4.  Once the cork is observed and approved, the waiter will pour a small amount of wine in the host's glass.

5.  The host will smell the wine to check the *bouquet,* which is the aroma of wine (pleasing to the smell).

6.  The host now swirls the wine to aerate the wine.

7.  If possible, the host will hold the glass of wine up against a white background to judge the color. Generally, tablecloths in fine restaurants are white. Look for a clear rather than muddy color in a red wine. Look for a light or a medium yellow in white wines.

8.  The host will take a small taste and gently swirl in his mouth to get the full flavor.

9.    Accepting the wine:
      If Acceptable: If the wine is acceptable, the host will say or
      nod his approval to the wine steward or waiter.

      If Unacceptable: If the wine is not acceptable, the host will
      ask to send it back. *Until the bottle is opened, no one knows for
      sure if the wine is good or if it is spoiled.*

      If in doubt, the waiter or wine steward may taste the wine
      to verify if it has, in fact, gone bad.

10.   After the taste test, all of the guests are served before the
      host is served.

11.   If the host is giving a toast, the sequence is as follows: 1) the
      host would test the wine first, 2) have the wine served to
      the guests, and 3) then served to himself. *The wine should be
      served to everyone before the host takes the first drink.*

12.   The host may now offer a toast to the guest of honor. (see
      The Toast section, pages 69-70)

13.   If the host is not going to give a toast (at this time), the host
      will then begin to drink the wine.

14.   Now everyone may drink the wine.

# THE TOAST

*Toasting* is believed to have come from the practice of placing a piece of burnt bread (toast) into the wine goblet to mellow the flavor of the wine. In days of old, a piece of toasted bread was put into the bottom of the glass and people drank until they got to the toast. Some believe the bread was used to help absorb (and help filter) the bad residue of the cheaper wines.

## GENERAL RULES

A toast is a few chosen words or sentences that congratulates, pays respect or pays tribute to a guest of honor, someone special, or a group (large or small).

**Do Not:**
- Do not give a "toast" to yourself if you are the recipient (or even a guest). This is considered the same as *applauding* yourself.

- Do not applaud at the end of a toast. The toast is the applause.

- Do not drink (any liquid, including water) *while* the toast is being given. Wait until immediately after the toast is given.

- The *recipient of the toast* does not drink to the toast because that would be considered the same as toasting (applauding) yourself.

- Do not rap the side of the stemware when toasting because the thin bowl of the stem might break and shatter. It happens!

- Do not use a toast as a personal opportunity to give a speech, no matter how much you want to. Do not use a toast to promote your own cause or agenda. A toast is not a speech.

- Do not make the toast about you. The toast is for and about the honoree(s).

## Do:

- Do give a short and simple toast. Do give a toast about the person you are toasting—not about yourself.

- A toast can be given at the start or the end of the meal.

- Do drink to a toast, but only after the toast has been given. You are not required to drink alcohol for it to be a proper toast. You can drink iced tea or soda instead. Note: some consider toasting with water bad luck.

- Do give the toast if you are the host. If you are not the host, you may give a toast, but only *after* the host. If the host is not comfortable with giving a toast, someone else may be assigned to give the toast.

- Do stand while giving the toast. It is appropriate for everyone but the recipient to stand.

- Do make eye contact with the guest of honor or recipient when the toast is being given. The audience should look towards the recipient.

- Do prepare a reciprocal toast if you're the recipient of the toast. Stand to give a reciprocal toast. (The others should be seated.)

- Do have a few *toasts* ready at all times such as:

> *"To the friendship of our companies and the longevity of our business relationship."*

> *"To your good health and pursuit of your dreams; may you have much success and happiness."*

> *"To the future relationship of our families and the joy of celebrations to come."*

# Section II: Dining Protocol

# E. BUSINESS ENTERTAINING

*"Entertaining is the opportunity to create a special memory for the host, the hostess, and the guests. The more each player fulfills his or her role, the better the event—and the memory."*

# BUSINESS ENTERTAINING

Entertaining is an important part of business. Any event such as dining (breakfast, coffee, lunch, brunch, or dinner) or networking with those you work with (or hope to work with) is business entertaining. Social protocol also applies to business entertaining.

Business entertaining includes: 1) a celebration, 2) a thank you to an individual or group, 3) an award or recognition, 4) the continuation of a business meeting or negotiation, and 5) to build or expand the business relationship.

**Reference Notes:**
- **Host:** *Refers to the host but also implies the hostess*

- **Dining In:** *Refers to entertaining in one's home or private club*

- **Dining Out:** *Any event where the guests order their own meal*

# ROLE OF THE HOST AND HOSTESS

The role of the host and the hostess is most important. Why? Because the host and hostess are the leaders who: 1) set the tone for the event, 2) guide and direct the process throughout the entire event, 3) make sure everyone is being included, and 4) make sure that everyone is having a good time.

The best events occur because the host and hostess leave nothing to chance. Successful events are dependent on the leaders (the host and hostess) to thoroughly prepare every detail from start to finish.

One of the biggest mistakes the host or hostess can make is that once the event starts, the host (or hostess) becomes *more of a guest than a host*. The successful host must be in charge from beginning to end; the host can still enjoy the event while fulfilling the responsibilities of the host or hostess.

# ROLE OF THE GUEST

The role of the guest is important because the success of the event also depends on the cooperation and attitude of the guests. The interaction between all of the guests is an important factor in any event. Guests who treat others with respect, use proper manners and good judgment, and add to the interest of any event are in high demand. Also, guests who are good conversationalists bring great value to building the business or social relationships.

The guests follow the example of the host and hostess for the sequence of events and the level of protocol. Always take your cue from the host or the hostess, whether in the home or at a facility.

For example, if the host and hostess want to have a more casual event, even though they are serving an elegant, formal meal in their home, they will demonstrate that through more casual attire dress code and through their behavior. Conversely, the host and hostess may exhibit formal behavior at a casual event. Some outdoor events, such as a barbeque, may be an upscale business–casual event rather than a shorts–and–tennis–shoes event.

Know that when events are held off–site (away from the office) it doesn't change the fact that business events are still about business.

# PLANNING THE EVENT

- Know and understand the type and purpose of the business event: celebration, award, reward or special tribute or simply to get together to build relationships.

- Will the event be casual, informal or formal? Sometimes companies host formal events just to observe who's comfortable and who is not in a formal setting. Some sponsor casual events to ensure the guests feel comfortable and relaxed.

## Who Pays?

- Dutch treat or hosted (the host or host organization pays for the event)? The person who invites is the person who pays for the event. Make it clear if you do not plan to pay. Do not ask a customer or client to pay—the vendor pays.

- For Dutch treat events (each person or company pays), tell the people when you invite them. For example, ask if the people can meet you for dinner at Blank Place where the entrées are around $15. Or just tell them this will be a Dutch treat event.

## Guest List

- How many? Which titles or positions will be included? Spouses or significant others included? Is there a guest of honor?

- Some savvy hosts determine the seating arrangement first to know the ideal number of guests, while others determine who they want to include and then decides on the best location.

## Dining In (Home) Location

- If you host the event in your home, will it be catered or home cooked by yourself or another person? If you are preparing the food and you are not a gourmet cook, select easy-to-prepare foods so you're not stuck in the kitchen. Be an available host.

## Dining Out Location

- Is it more convenient for both the guests and the host to have the event at a restaurant, private club, or other facility? Popular restaurants book weeks and months in advance. Start early to get the reservations you want.

## Working with the Facility

- Have a written contract. Be clear on every aspect of the event: number of guests, selected room or table location, table and place settings, table decorations, menu, payment arrangements, time to start and end, and any other special needs.

- Call a week before the event to verify the restaurant or facility is still able to meet your needs and requests. Call the day before the event to further verify all details. Leave nothing to chance.

- Many private clubs do not allow papers on the tables during lunch or dinner. Verify your private club rules in advance.

## Working with the Caterer
- Today, many home events use a caterer to set up, provide and serve the meal, and clean up. Always check caterer references.

## Seating Arrangements
- Decide the seating arrangement in advance. If you do not use place cards, tell the guests where you would like for them to sit.

## SPECIAL NEEDS OF GUESTS

The considerate host or hostess will ask the guests in advance if they have any food preferences or issues such as allergies, religious food issues, or if they are a vegetarian.

## THE VEGETARIAN

### The Host
- Years ago, the vegetarian was the lone person at the table with special food needs. Today, the business or social host needs to be aware and considerate of the guest's food needs.

- Some event planners now estimate and plan for 20 percent of the attendees to request a vegetarian meal, whether because of health, religion, or because of the appeal of the vegetarian meal.

- When possible, ask in advance if the guests have special food requirements or include the request in the invitation. For formal written invitations, this request is more difficult.

- As a safeguard, be prepared with vegetarian choices: fruits, vegetables, and no-meat pasta dishes. Some vegetarians eat fish; some eat dairy, some eat eggs, and some eat fowl.

- For corporate events, always offer an optional vegetarian main course. Today, most event planners ask attendees for food preferences prior to the event.

### The Vegetarian Guest
- Corporate events: If you have not been asked your food preference, notify your event contact before the event that you are vegetarian or have special food needs.

- Plan ahead. If you think the at-home host will not be offering vegetarian options, you may wish to eat a light snack before you go. Unfortunately, there are situations the vegetarian has no control over (and should not try to control) the food.

- Communicate: When you RSVP by telephone or in writing, you may wish to indicate you are a vegetarian or have allergies.

## GUESTS WITH DISABILITIES

### The Host
- Are there any guests with disabilities? Are the steps too steep or are there hand rails? Is there a wheelchair ramp or elevator? Are the doors and aisles (paths of travel) wide enough for a wheelchair? (see Accommodating Guests with Disabilities, pages 135-136)

- The considerate host and hostess will learn about any issues before the event to ensure everyone is comfortable and safe.

### The Guest
- If you have special needs unknown to the host or hostess, please let them know in advance. Please do not wait until you arrive.

# THE INVITATION

## The Host

- The level of desired formality of the event guides the selection of the type of invitation: handwritten, calligraphy, e-mail, telephone call, or engraved-formal invitation.

- Include the date, beginning and ending time, location (with map), host information, RSVP instructions, and dress code.

## The Guest

- RSVP as soon as you know you can or cannot attend. The host doesn't know you can come or not unless you tell him or her. The biggest complaints of event planners and hosts are that many guests: 1) never respond they will not attend, 2) show up without a response, or 3) the guest RSVPs after the facility deadlines have passed and the guest count is turned in.

- Once you've determined you can attend, make sure you have the appropriate attire. Do not wait until it's too late to react to discover you do not have the appropriate clothing.

# ARRIVING AT THE EVENT

## The Host

- Dining Out: Arrive before your guests. Meet with the waiters assigned to your event and let them know you are the host. Let the waiters know your expectations and any special requests.

- Dining Out: Arrive early to check the table location, the table and place settings, decorations, and to place the place cards.

- Dining Out: If you have ordered a special cake, ask to see it before the meal to verify the cake, decorations and writing (if any) is what you have ordered. Wrong cakes and wrong decorations happen.

- Dining In: Always greet and welcome your guests with gracious hospitality. Don't be or appear frazzled even though you may have many last-minute preparations. Relax and enjoy.

- Dining In: The gracious host and hostess are ready *before* the guests arrive. Plan to be early at your own party.

## The Guest

- The attitude of the arriving guests also sets the tone for the entire event. Arrive in a pleasant and positive mood.

- Before you leave for the event, have the correct address, map with instructions, and the facility and host's phone number. Leave in plenty of time to assure you will not be late.

- Turn off your cell phone *before* you arrive.

- Dining In: Arrive on time; promptness is not only proper, it is appreciated. When the event is held in someone's home, arriving too early can be an imposition on the host—especially if the host is not ready. If you arrive early at the host's home, wait until the appointed time to knock on the door.

- Dining In: Being late can ruin the serving schedule as well as the food. The host who is preparing the food has timed the food to be ready at a specific time. If you have an emergency and cannot help being late, call and let the host know. Insist they start without you if you're late.

## GREETING THE GUESTS

## The Host

- The initial greeting by the host and hostess helps to set the tone for the entire event. Greet the guests with a warm, friendly welcome. A positive attitude is your greatest asset. Treat everyone as if he or she is the most special person attending.

- Be prepared to introduce all the guests. Know how to pronounce each person's name and know something of interest about each person. The more information you can share about your guests, the faster they will connect with each other.

- Dining In: If possible, the host or hostess or both should greet the guests as they arrive. When entertaining in the home without outside help, it's not unusual for the host or hostess to be finishing the preparations or visiting with other guests. The host and hostess should stand close to the entry area to ensure a personal greeting to all the guests.

- Dining Out: Wait in the lobby or dining area to greet your guests. If you are not in the lobby, make sure someone is there to greet and direct the guests to your table.

- Dining Out: Stand to greet the guests until all have arrived.

- Dining Out: Direct the guests to their correct seats. If, for some reason, a guest sits in the wrong place, just leave him there unless you have a guest of honor who should be in that seat.

**The Guest**
- Remember that the role of the guest is as important to a successful event as the role of the host.

- The guests should start mingling and meeting the other guests after they have said hello to the host and hostess.

## HOST OR HOSTESS GIFT

**The Host**
- When receiving a hostess gift, be sure to admire it and verbally thank them. In case the guest did not include a card, make a mental note of which guest brought which gift.

- Dining In: If you receive wine as a hostess gift but have already selected wine for the meal, just say, "Thank you so much, we'll enjoy this special bottle later."

- A thank you note for the hostess gift is not required, but for that special hostess gift, a thank you note is always appreciated.

## The Guest

- Be thoughtful in your selection. Choose something appropriate and moderate in price. Select a generic hostess gift for someone you do not know well. Generic gifts include a non-controversial book, candy, wine, flowers, or a nice candle.

- Dining In: Taking a small gift to the host who is entertaining in his home is a gesture of courtesy and appreciation. Remember, giving a hostess gift when you arrive is not a substitute for the handwritten thank you note to be sent after the event.

- Dining In: If you take a bottle of wine, do not be disappointed if your wine is not served at the event. The host will have already selected the appropriate wines for the meal or event.

- Dining In: Bring fresh flowers already arranged in a vase to avoid additional work by the host. A guest would not want to have the host have to find a vase, cut, and arrange the flowers.

## PRE-DINNER DRINKS

## The Host

- The cocktail time is to help transition the guests from their arrival to the main event. Because it can be an indicator of the success of the event, the cocktail time plays an important part. Generally, if the guests are having a good time during the cocktail time, they will continue to enjoy the rest of the event.

- Set a specific time for serving pre-dinner drinks. Too many drinks and hors d'oeuvres can spoil the guests' appetite—and the dinner. Limit the number of appetizers and keep it simple.

- Watch for those who may be drinking too much. The wiped-out guest can ruin the evening, not to mention any possible liabilities after he or she leaves your home or the facility.

- The host and hostess can help set the example on alcohol consumption. So, if you're the host or hostess, be aware of how much you drink.

- End the cocktail time several minutes before dinner to allow for a smooth transition from cocktails to the meal or main event.

- Dining In: Choose whether to serve: 1) an alcoholic punch, 2) no alcohol, 3) wine and beer only, 4) wine only, or 5) a full bar. For a full bar, have an assortment of selected beverages, mixers, garnishes, plenty of ice, napkins, and stirrers.

- Dining In: Some hosts prefer to hire a professional bartender to tend bar so the host and hostess are free to visit with the guests.

- Dining In: To help reduce alcohol consumption, stock up on water, sodas, and non-alcoholic beverages. An unattended open bar encourages increased alcohol consumption. Have a designated bartender or ask a colleague to help serve drinks.

- Dining Out: Some organizations do not offer a hosted bar (host picks up the drink tab) to discourage heavy drinking before the business or social event.

## The Guest
- The cocktail time is important because it is a form of networking, whether for business or social purposes. This is a great opportunity to meet others before the main event.

- If this is a large gathering, the cocktail time helps to provide the opportunity for the guests to become acquainted and to visit with everyone. Be friendly and work the crowd. Learn each guest's first *and* last name and something about them.

- If this is a business gathering, keep a business mindset. Relax and have fun, but retain your professional persona.

- Protect your good judgment. Drink slowly and know your limit. Know how many drinks you will have for the entire evening. Avoid over drinking; too many drinks can drown you and your career.

- If you arrive thirsty, be sure to quench your thirst with water, club soda, or a soft drink to prevent consuming too much alcohol too quickly.

- Dilute alcohol consumption by selecting a light beer, a wine spritzer (which is wine mixed with club soda), or by lowering the alcohol-to-mixer ratio on mixed drinks.

- Remember to hold a cold or iced beverage in your left hand, keeping the right hand warm and dry for shaking hands.

## SEATING ARRANGEMENTS

**The Host**
- The right seating arrangement will enhance any party. Always plan the seating arrangement to maximize the guest interaction and to encourage interesting conversations. Seat those who are shy next to those who are not.

- Use place cards to ensure the guests are seated as you wish. Unless there are unusual circumstances, spouses or couples are not seated next to each other.

- A round table, especially a large one, works best if you seat rank side by side or close together. In large gatherings, a table for 10 makes it almost impossible to talk with those across the table.

- When entertaining by yourself, ask someone to serve as your co-host. Most colleagues or even guests will be glad to help.

## SEATING DIAGRAM – RECTANGULAR TABLE

The host sits at one end and the hostess sits at the opposite end of a *rectangular table*.

The guest of honor (1-in diagram below) sits at the right side of the host and the person who accompanied the guest of honor (2) sits at the right side of the hostess.

The next ranking person (3) sits on the left side of the host and the next ranking person (4) sits on the left of the hostess.

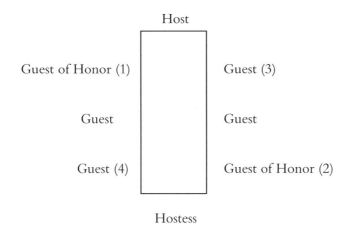

## The Guest

- When the host announces that dinner is ready to be served, the guests should take their places as soon as possible.

- Do whatever you need to do before taking your seat at the table. Make any quick calls, use the restroom, or double check your hair and makeup before the meal begins.

- Never rearrange the place cards. The host or hostess has placed the cards there for a reason—to ensure the success of the event.

- If there are no place cards, wait until the hostess indicates where you are to sit. If the hostess sits down without designating a place for you, then sit in a chair close or convenient to you.

- Greet the other guests at your table. Try to remember and use each person's first name in conversation. Nothing is more important to a person than his or her name.

- A gentleman still helps a lady to be seated and still opens the door for a lady. Gentlemen still stand or rise (slightly) from their chair when a lady leaves and returns to the table.

- Dining In: Once the hostess is seated, place your napkin on your lap or when the hostess places her napkin on her lap.

- Do not lean back in the chair. You could fall or even break the chair—it happens. Do not push your chair back and cross your legs in a casual pose during the meal or between courses.

- Use good posture. Sit up straight at the table; do not lean on the table. Correct posture always improves one's appearance.

- If you are seated close to any of the food dishes, the host may ask you to help pass or serve the dish.

# BEFORE THE MEAL

## The Host

- Never forget—it is always about the guests. The prepared host and hostess help to make the transition from the cocktail hour to the main meal easy, smooth and comfortable for the guests.

- Dining In: Before the guests are seated, make sure the table is set, the water glasses are filled, the serving pieces are in place, the place cards are properly placed, the candles are lit, and the room temperature comfortable.

- Dining In: Serve each food course at the appointed time. Serve hot foods hot and cold foods cold. Invest in warming trays or insulated servers to help keep food warm.

- Dining In: Be ready to be seated when you ask your guests to be seated. The role of the host is important in the transition of the cocktail time and the seating time.

# ORDERING (Dining Out)

## The Host

- One way to let the waiter know you are the host is to *take the lead in ordering process*. Start the ordering by turning to the guest of honor (seated to your right), and say, "*Guest of Honor_____, why don't you start?*"

- The host orders last. The host should discretely ask the server (waiter or waitress) if everyone has ordered certain courses, such as a salad and a soup. So the "table" is eating the same number of courses, the host may then encourage (without insisting) those who did not previously order these courses to do so.

- The host should never let a guest eat alone. Even if only one guest orders an additional course(s), the host may also order the course(s) so the guest is not eating alone.

- To start the meal, the host may order a selection of appetizers for the table to share. The host would order these first and then the guests can order the rest of their meal.

- To ensure guests feel comfortable in ordering what they want, the host or the hostess may say, "Let's all enjoy an appetizer (or soup or salad). The shrimp cocktail here is outstanding."

## The Guest
- One never goes wrong in ordering easy-to-eat foods. When it comes to price, you are safe if you order a meal that is neither the most expensive nor the cheapest.

- Ideally, to keep the timing of courses on track, the group should be ordering a similar number of courses. Guests should pay attention to what the others are ordering.

- Guests, when ordering, can quietly ask the waiter what courses others are ordering so they order a similar number of courses.

- A guest would not want to sit out the appetizer, soup, or salad while others are eating these courses. Conversely, a guest should not order five courses if everyone else is only ordering two.

- Normally, the guest of honor (regardless of gender) orders first, then the women and then the men. The host always orders last. Alternatively, after the guest of honor orders, the rest of the table can order counter-clockwise ending with the host.

- The host selects and tastes the wines. Unless you (the guest) are asked to help with the wine selection, do not offer. The host may have a budget and may want to control the wine selection. (see Wine section, pages 65-68)

# THE MEAL BEGINS

## The Host

- The host and hostess are responsible for making sure the food and condiments are passed to everyone. A gracious host or hostess keeps alert to the wants and needs of the guests throughout the entire meal to make sure all is well.

- The host makes sure the bread, butter, and condiments are passed around the table. The host can direct the waiter to replenish the beverages, bread, butter, or condiments as needed.

- Too much *watching over* by a host or hostess can be obtrusive, while too little is neglectful.

- Since the guests are not to start eating until the hostess has taken the first bite, make sure you (the hostess) are at the table and not in the kitchen while everyone is waiting for you to start.

- The hostess should check to see if everyone has been served before taking the first bite of food.

- Some hosts will ask the guest of honor to start the eating process. If there is no guest of honor, the host starts.

- This is an area where there is recent debate; some believe that the guest should start eating when served. I still believe there should be order in dining and that it is best when everyone is eating at the same time and finishing close to the same time.

## The Guest

- Wait to eat until everyone is served. Be patient for the food and condiments to be passed.

- Wait for the hostess to start. The hostess is the first one to start eating and the last one to finish eating.

- If you are missing flatware or a napkin, do not substitute; ask the waiter or your hostess for the missing flatware or napkin.

## DURING THE MEAL – GENERAL DINING MANNERS

### The Host and Guests

- Eat slowly. In our fast-paced culture we often rush too fast through a meal. Relax, take your time, and enjoy the meal.

- Take small bites. Put your fork down and pause between bites. Always be available for conversation during the meal.

- Do not talk with food in your mouth; it just looks bad. Chew with your mouth closed. Do not make noises while chewing.

- Do not play with your food or the flatware or stemware at the table. Do not dunk food into a beverage. Do not *double dip*, which is dipping food in a group dish twice.

- If you do not like a food(s) served, do not make it public. Simply leave it on your plate. Avoid drawing attention.

- Bad bite: take your napkin to your mouth and place the morsel in your napkin. Place it discreetly on the plate at the end of the meal or course. Placing a bad bite back on your plate during the meal leaves a most unpleasant sight.

- Your hands may rest on your lap or on the edge of the table. Elbows do not belong on the table. Keep your elbows close to your side when you cut your food. Your forearms may rest against the edge of the table in less formal settings.

- Do not make inappropriate noises, such as burping, belching, slurping, chewing loudly, or drumming your fingers.

- Do not apply makeup other than lipstick at the table. Apply lipstick quickly and discreetly. If you have to apply lip liner and lip gloss, do so in the powder room. Do not touch or comb your hair (or anyone else's hair) during the meal. It's considered unsanitary.

- Do not place used or dirty flatware on the table. If possible, place the flatware on a dish, a saucer, or the under-plate.

- If coughing hard or sneezing, excuse yourself and leave the table. Return to the table as soon as possible. Avoid making comments about it when you return.

- Avoid being loud or boisterous, which is disruptive and annoying to the other diners in the restaurant.

## CONVERSATION

### The Host
- A good host makes sure the guests are having a good time. Although it's the responsibility of each guest to participate in conversation, the host makes sure everyone is included.

- If the conversation becomes too serious or too intense for the guests and the occasion, change the subject graciously. Help save face (prevent embarrassment or hurt feelings) for those involved.

- The gracious host is aware of who is engaged in conversation and who is not. Make sure everyone appears included. The host or hostess should pick up the slack if the conversation subsides.

### The Host and Guests
- Courtesy words and phrases are the basics of good manners. Generously use words such as: "Please," "Thank you," "You're welcome" and "Excuse me."

- Know the difference between meals for fellowship and entertaining from meals that are primarily for nourishment during the course of business. Sometimes, a business discussion is the primary focus and the meal is secondary.

- If the client wishes to discuss business during the meal, then the host would defer to the client.

- If business is discussed, it is usually not discussed until coffee and dessert, or the end of the meal.

- Avoid gossip, condescending remarks about others, gender bashing, or other controversial topics.

- Do not interrupt others while they are talking. Learn to listen. A good listener is considered to be more articulate and intelligent than the talker!

- Start a conversation with "Hello, my name is…what's yours?

- Questions are the best way to engage your dinner companions. The questions should be friendly and easy to understand. Avoid questions that are too personal or inappropriate.

- Avoid asking others about their marital status, income level, how much they pay for taxes or other proprietary questions.

- Shy people may have a difficult time engaging in social conversation at a business meeting, so don't mistake a person as being aloof when they are actually just very shy.

- Shyness affects a large percentage of our population. If you are shy, try hard to participate. Learn to ask questions about the *other person*. Remember, many of the top managers and business leaders consider themselves shy.

- If you are not shy, make an effort to include those who are.

- Always look people in the eye (in our culture) when having a conversation. You appear more interested. The more interested the listener, the more the talker will want to talk.

- Do not tell dirty, inappropriate, or distasteful jokes. Avoid controversial topics such as religion, gender issues, or politics.

## SECOND SERVINGS

### The Host
- Dining In: A good idea, but not required, is for the hostess to cook or order extra just in case the guests are unusually hungry or one of your dishes is an exceptionally big hit.

- Dining In: Offer extra servings only if there is enough food for everyone to have seconds. If a guest asks for seconds and there are none, simply say, "I'm sorry there is no more, but I'm so glad you enjoyed it!"

- Dining In: When it comes to second servings of the main dish, the wise hostess will cut the extra into smaller pieces so more guests may have a second serving if they wish.

### The Guest
- Dining In: The guest's request for a second serving can be a great compliment—especially if there is enough food to provide a second serving. If not, the request can be a great source of embarrassment to the host and the guest.

- Dining In: The guideline is to wait until the host or hostess offers the option of a second serving. If seconds are not offered, the guest should not ask.

- Whether dining in or out, even if the guest can see on the serving platter that there is more food, the guest should still wait for the host or hostess to offer the extra food to the guests.

- Dining In: Some hostesses will not offer seconds unless there is enough to offer everyone a second serving. This avoids partiality as to who gets the last serving.

## CLEARING THE TABLE

### The Host
- The person clearing the table should not reach across and in front of the person at that place setting. The dinner plate and drinks are removed from the right, and the salad plate and the bread and butter plate are removed from the left.

### The Guest
- It is not proper to stack your dirty dishes.

- Dining In: Although it may be a kind gesture to offer to help clear the table (non-formal meals), if the hostess declines, then visit with the others at the table.

## THE ENDING OF THE MEAL

### The Host
- The host and hostess now begin the transition from the end of the meal to the end of the event. This transition time can be a good time to serve the guests another cup of coffee or tea.

- The role of the host continues. Keep the conversation going until the last person eating has finished. Never rush the guests. But if that rare guest is staying much longer than appropriate for that event, the host can say, "Unfortunately, we have an early morning tomorrow, but we have truly enjoyed our visit with you." Whatever you choose to say, say it with a kind tone.

- For a formal ending, the host may stand and thank everyone for coming. Always thank your guests, regardless of formality.

- Dining In: The candles stay lit until the guests have left, unless the candles have burned down too low and pose a fire risk.

- Dining In: Avoid turning on the television, showing family movies, or coercing guests into an unwanted parlor game.

- Dining In: Wait until the guests have left before clearing the table of the dessert and coffee service.

## The Guest

- When you are finished eating, place your fork and knife (blade towards the center of the plate) together in a diagonal position on your plate in the five o'clock position. (see pages 56–57)

- Do not use a toothpick or pick your teeth at the table.

- Leaving immediately after the meal has an *eat and run* effect so take time to visit afterwards. To leave too early *or* too late can insult the host. Observe the host and hostess for signs of when the event is beginning to end.

## TAKING FOOD HOME

### The Host
- Dining In: If this is a casual gathering and you have lots of food left, you may want to offer (although not expected) the guests a gift bag of food to take home. Do this only if you have enough for each guest to take something and only if you have sturdy containers that can be safely sealed to avoid any spills.

### The Guest
- Dining In: Taking a doggie bag is a tough decision. Take only if the host has offered and, even then, understand the downside if you do; possible spills or poor image of taking a doggie bag from someone's home. Understand the downside if you do not take it; the hostess may be offended.

## PAYING THE BILL (Dining Out)

### The Host

- Always review the bill (or tab) when you receive it. Double check that it is your bill and that the bill is accurate.

- Add the gratuity quickly and discretely. Do not use your calculator to figure the tip. (see Tipping, pages 117 and 153)

- Make sure your credit card is valid before you arrive at the restaurant or that you have sufficient cash. Some restaurants only accept cash or certain credit cards.

- To avoid any hassle over payment: 1) give your credit card to the waiter in advance, 2) specify the gratuity percentage, and 3) have the waiter give you the completed receipt at the end.

- If you have any concerns about the safety of your identity through your credit card, you may choose to pay in cash. If you do, have sufficient cash with you.

### The Guest

- The guest does not pay. If you (the guest) feel you must offer to help cover the costs, offer only once. If the host declines your offer, please don't push. Genuinely offering once is sufficient.

## THE END OF THE EVENT

### The Host

- Dining In: If you want the guests to stay, say so and mean it. Lead a spirited discussion or have meaningful activities or topics in mind for after the meal.

- Dining In: Conversely, do not be so anxious for the guests to leave that you ruin your own party—even if you are really tired. Most will notice if the host has zoned out of the event.

- Dining In: Have a plan for ending the party. What will be the transition from the dinner to the end? Will you offer activities after the meal or just conversation? Decide which room will be the end-of-the-party room.

- Dining In: It is improper to quickly end the party at the end of the meal. Allow an appropriate time for final conversation.

- No matter whether your guests exhibit good manners or rudeness, you ultimately are responsible for setting the example.

## SAYING GOODBYE

### The Host
- Dining In: Thank your guests for coming. Walk each one to the door or remain at the door to say good-bye to each guest as they leave.

- Look at each guest in the eye and focus on each guest as they leave. The farewell to your guest is as important as the initial greeting. Your voice and eyes should be friendly and warm.

- Dining In: Unless the lit candles are burning dangerously low, blow the candles out after the last guest has left.

### The Guest
- Leave at an appropriate or at the appointed time.

- Do not rush to leave too fast after the meal. It may send a message to the host that you did not have a good time.

- Never leave a party or event without saying goodbye to the host and hostess. Be sure to thank both the host and hostess for their hospitality.

- Say goodbye to the other guests, especially the guest of honor.

- To overstay your welcome may eliminate you from the next party list. You may want to wait until after a few guests have left before you to start your exit.

## AFTER THE EVENT

### The Host
- Send a thank you note or at least call the caterer or facility if you were pleased with the outcome. The wise host knows the value of a good relationship with vendors and facilities.

### The Guest
- The verbal thank you when you leave does not replace the handwritten note.

- Always send a thank you card within 24 hours. An e-mail message is better than nothing, but does not carry the same significance of a handwritten note.

- A telephone call (in addition to the note) the next day or two to the hostess is always appreciated.

- What if? If you have not sent a thank you note within a reasonable amount of time, call the hostess and apologize for the delay; thank them and then send a note immediately.

# Section II: Dining Protocol

# F. CHALLENGING FOODS – GENERAL

*"Challenging foods—just as any challenging task—simply require understanding and practicing the guidelines."*

## CHALLENGES WITH APPETIZERS

- **FINGER FOODS:** If the finger food is larger than one bite, eat only if you can eat without spilling, dripping, or spraying.

- **STICKY or GREASY FINGER FOODS:** Avoid any messy finger foods. You will not be able to shake hands with a clean hand unless you go wash your hands first. These messy foods are just not worth it at a business (or social) gathering.

- **HORS D'OEUVRES HOLDERS-TOOTHPICKS:** Place used holders or toothpicks in your napkin and leave in an appropriate waste container. Do not place a dirty holder back on the appetizer tray or table.

- **GARNISHES:** Garnishes enhance the look of the appetizer and should be edible. When in doubt, don't eat the garnish.

- **JUGGLING DRINK and PLATE:** Before you get yourself burdened down with beverage, food plate, purse or briefcase; make sure there will be a place to set your glass or plate.

  Alternate eating and drinking, which will leave your right hand clean and free to shake hands.

- **DIPS:** Do not double-dip a chip, a vegetable, or any other food item into a community dip or sauce. When in doubt, do not eat the dip. Runny dips can be disasters. Salsa does not look great on light-colored clothes.

- **SKEWERS:** Slide all the food off the wooden skewer or kabob with your fork onto your plate. This also applies to skewered entrées. Eat the food with your fork (and knife).

## CHALLENGES WITH BREAD AND ROLLS

- **BREAD and BUTTER PLATE:** Place one serving of bread on your bread and butter (B and B plate) plate. Put a serving of butter or spread with the butter knife onto your B and B plate.

  If there is no bread and butter plate, place your bread or roll on the left side of your dinner plate. If there is no bread and butter plate in a casual setting, such as an informal Italian restaurant, you may place the dinner roll on the table (with a clean tablecloth) on the left side of the dinner plate. You can always ask for a small plate. Take your cue from the host/hostess.

- **BUTTER KNIFE:** Generally shaped like a small saber, the butter knife remains with the butter dish or the spread that is passed around the table. Pass the butter knife *with* the butter.

- **BUTTER SPREADER:** The individual butter spreader stays on your bread and butter plate for your own use.

- **BREADSTICKS:** Hold a breadstick with your fingers to eat. Place the breadstick on your bread and butter plate.

- **BREAD or ROLL:** Break the roll into one bite-size piece with your fingers. Butter the bite-size piece with your spreader or knife and eat. Do this with one piece of bread at a time.

- **TOAST:** Cut toast diagonally in half. The halves may be completely buttered and eaten in several bites. You do not have to break toast into bite-size pieces before eating.

- **BAGUETTES:** If a baguette is not cut completely through, use a clean napkin to hold the baguette and avoid touching the bread with your hands while you tear or cut a serving.

# CHALLENGES WITH COCKTAILS

- **STIRRERS:** Do not leave a cocktail stirrer in the glass; you could accidentally poke yourself in the eye. Stir the drink and leave the stirrer in the trash receptacle by the bar or bar station.

- **GARNISHES:** Lemons, limes, olives, or fruit slices add a touch of color and flavor to drinks. Do not eat the garnish unless the garnish is edible, such as an olive, mint leaf, maraschino cherry, or pickled onion. The raw peel of a lemon or lime is not edible. When in doubt, don't eat the garnish.

- **NUMBER of DRINKS:** Know your limit. The more you lose control and good judgment, the more your career and even your personal life can be negatively affected.

- **ICE in DRINKS:** Do not chew or suck on ice.

- **PARASOLS:** Dispose of the parasol before you drink the cocktail. It's for looks and does not enhance the beverage.

- **ICE BUCKET and TONGS:** Always use tongs or a large spoon to get ice. Do not use your hands to retrieve ice.

- **BEER in CANS or BOTTLES:** Ask for a glass for your beer unless at a casual gathering. Take your cue from the host and hostess whether to drink from a glass or the beer can or bottle.

- **COASTERS:** Do not set a cocktail glass on wood furniture or a marble top without a coaster. Neither cloth nor paper napkins can protect marble or a wood furniture finish. Genuine marble stains very easily. This is not the way to leave your mark!

- **NAPKINS:** Keep several napkins wrapped around a cold iced drink to keep your hand from being wet and cold.

## CHALLENGES WITH RELISHES

- **CHUTNEY:** Place the chutney on your dinner, salad, or bread and butter plate. Chutney is eaten with a fork or spoon.

- **PREPARED RELISHES:** Place hot dog and hamburger relish directly on the food in very casual settings, such as an outdoor picnic. However, in formal settings, it's best to place the relish on your plate first, then on the hot dog or hamburger.

- **OLIVES:** Bite carefully into olives with pits. Remove the pit by placing it on your fork or spoon and onto your plate. Pitted olives may be stuffed with pimento, garlic, almonds, etc.

- **PICKLED FOODS:** Eat pickled foods with a salad fork.

- **RAW VEGETABLES:** Remove the raw vegetable(s) from the serving plate to your plate, preferably with a serving piece. Raw vegetables are finger food and held with your fingers.

- **RELISH TRAY:** Use the available serving piece to take the relish from the relish tray and place on your salad or bread and butter plate. Relishes usually are eaten with a fork or spoon.

- **SALSA:** Be careful with thin salsas because thin salsa drips easily. If possible, place a serving of salsa on your plate rather than dip from the community serving bowl. Don't double dip.

*Note: Relishes and pickled or other acid foods will pit sterling silver if left in contact for a long time. Do not leave sterling silverware in acidic foods. Rinse these utensils with soap and water as soon as possible to help prevent any irreparable damage.*

# CHALLENGES WITH SALADS

- **EATING the SALAD:** The biggest challenge is often in eating the large leaves of lettuce or greens. Too often facilities do not serve the lettuce or salad greens in bite-size pieces.

  Use a salad fork and knife to cut a salad that is served on a plate in front of you. Cut a salad that is served on your left side with a fork, if only to avoid the difficulty of cutting the left-side salad with a knife and a fork.

  Never cut the entire salad at one time; it's permissible to cut a few bites (three to four) at a time.

- **ENTRÉE SALADS:** An entrée salad, the main course of the meal, is larger than a side salad. A chicken Caesar salad is a good example of an entrée salad.

- Use your luncheon or dinner fork (not the salad fork) for an entrée salad. If a salad fork for a side (smaller) salad is not provided, ask the waiter for a salad fork. At someone's home, follow the cue of the host/hostess. If they use a regular fork, then follow suit.

- **SALAD DRESSING:** Avoid soaking your salad with too much dressing. If you use lemon slices as a dressing, cup your hand over the lemon to prevent squirting your neighbor.

- **CHERRY TOMATOES:** Avoid putting a whole cherry tomato or small tomato in your mouth. Cut with a fork and knife before eating. Pierce the tomato with the tine or prong of the fork, and cut in half with your knife. Piercing with one of the end fork tines makes it easier to pierce. If you are having trouble piercing through a tough tomato skin, just leave the cherry tomato on the salad plate as a beautiful decoration.

# CHALLENGES WITH SOUPS

- **THE SOUP COURSE:** Soup is often served at formal meals, making it essential to the rising high-ranking executive that he or she be able to eat this difficult food properly. Bouillon is especially difficult because it's so thin. Simply practice eating soup until you get it right.

- **SOUP SPOONS:** To eat soup, scoop the soup into the soup spoon *away from you;* towards the back of the soup bowl.

  Eat soup from the side of the soup spoon; do not place the entire bowl of the spoon in your mouth. Be careful not to overfill the spoon to prevent spilling. Soup takes time (and focus) to eat properly.

  The bouillon soup spoon is round and used for clear soup. A cream soup spoon is also round, but with a deeper bowl. The gumbo spoon is oval with a deep bowl and is used for either thick or cream soups. Teaspoons are too small for soup.

- **SOUP SPOON PLACEMENT–Cups and Bowls:** While eating (and when finished) soup from a cup or small bowl, place the soup spoon on the under-plate.

- **SOUP SPOON PLACEMENT–Rimmed Soup Plate:** While eating (and when finished), soup from a rimmed soup plate, keep the spoon in the rimmed soup plate with the handle of the spoon rested on the edge (rim) rather than on the under-plate.

- **SOUP BOWL:** Soup served in Asian-style soup bowls can be drunk after any solids have been eaten with the spoon first. Use both hands to hold the soup bowl when drinking the soup.

- **SOUP BOWLS with HANDLES:** Small cups and bowls of soup with one or two handles can be drunk from the bowl or cup rather than with a spoon. If there are solid pieces of food in the soup, use the spoon to eat the solid pieces first before drinking the liquid. Hold with the handles to drink.

- **COOLING the SOUP:** Do not slurp or blow on soup to cool. Skim the top of the soup at the edges or rim, which is the coolest area, or simply wait until the soup has cooled down.

- **EATING SOUP:** It is permissible to tip the bowl or cup back to get the last spoonful. However, sometimes it looks better to just leave the last few drops rather than to tip the bowl. Why? Because most people don't know this is permissible and may wonder why you are so hungry that you have to tip the bowl back to get to the very last drop.

- **CRACKERS and BREAD:** Do not put crumbled crackers in the soup. If you really like crushed crackers or bread in your soup, save this for your "at home" manners. Croutons are appropriate, as is the crouton or toast in French onion soup.

  If you are eating crackers with soup, do not eat double fisted, which is eating with the soup spoon in the right hand and a cracker in the left hand at the same time. Use the same hand to eat either the soup or the crackers.

- **OYSTER CRACKERS:** Oyster crackers (not crumbled) are appropriate to put in soup, especially in clam or oyster soup or chowder. This is one exception to the above rule.

- **FOOD TO FACE:** Soup, especially thin soup, is one of the foods considered most difficult to eat. Just because a food is difficult does not lessen the rules of etiquette. Rather than place your face close to the soup, maintain your correct body posture (sit up straight) and bring the soup spoon to your face.

# Section II: Dining Protocol

# G. CHALLENGING FOODS – SPECIFIC

*"Foods require certain methods of cooking and preparation,
just as foods require certain methods of consumption."*

## HOW TO EAT SPECIFIC FOODS

**ARTICHOKE:** Artichoke leaves are properly eaten with one's fingers. Remove each leaf and dip the bottom part of the leaf (the part that is closest to the base or heart of the artichoke) into the sauce and scrape the meat of the artichoke off with your teeth.

Discard the leaf in a designated plate. When all the leaves are eaten, cut and eat the heart with a fork and knife. Do not eat the hairy choke of the artichoke or the fibrous part of the artichoke leaf.

**BACON:** Crisp bacon is easy to eat with your fingers, but it's messy. Try cutting with your knife without catapulting the bacon.

**CAKE, REGULAR:** Eat regular cake with a dessert fork.

**CAKE, POUND:** Pound cake may be eaten with your fingers, but in a formal setting use the dessert fork.

**CAKE, PETIT FOUR:** When removing a petit four cake from the serving plate, remove with the service piece. If it is served with a wrapper, remove the wrapper before eating.

Eat the petit four with your fingers or with a fork, depending on the formality of the event. If the sides are moist or messy, or you are in doubt as to how to eat the petit four, use a fork.

**CELERY, RAW:** Eat raw celery with your fingers. Take small bites and crunch as quietly as you can. If you order celery hearts from a menu, be sure to ask how the celery hearts will be prepared. If the celery hearts are not cooked, you'll be crunching raw celery.

**CHICKEN, FRIED:** Eat fried chicken with your fingers at a casual gathering. For a formal meal one would use the fork and knife to cut fried chicken. For those rare occasions when fried chicken is served at a formal meal, be careful and use your napkin to keep your hands (and mouth) clean.

106

**CORNISH HEN:** The Cornish hen, a small fowl, is carved similarly as a turkey is carved. Carve and eat (with a fork and knife) one side of the Cornish hen before you carve and eat the next side.

**To Carve a Cornish Hen:**
1.  Remove the thigh–leg section as one piece by separating at the connecting joint of the thigh and body. Use the fork and knife to probe to find the thigh–leg joint.

2.  Separate the thigh from the leg at the connecting joint with the fork and knife. It should cut easily once you're at the joint.

3.  Separate the wing from the thigh at its connecting joint. If you do not plan to eat the thigh or wing, you can skip this step.

4.  The breast of the Cornish hen can now be cut into slices. Some will carve the breast across the bottom of the breast and then carve the breast away from the breastbone so it comes off in one piece. Then the whole breast can be carved in pieces.

    Generally there is little room to carve the breast on the dinner plate, so the breast is sliced directly from the breastbone.

**To Eat a Cornish Hen:**
1.  You may eat each piece as it is carved.

2.  If you do not want to eat the leg, thigh or wing, you may carve these pieces, set it aside and just slice the breast to eat.

3.  In a casual setting, you may eat the wing or leg with your fingers. In a formal meal, although permissible, I recommend you use only the fork and knife just so you keep you hands clean. There might not be a finger bowl afterwards!

4.  Always take your cue from the host or hostess and follow suit. Watch how they or carving and eating the Cornish hen.

**CORN ON THE COB, CASUAL:** Use corn holders or toothpicks to hold the cob. Holding the cob with your fingers can be too messy, especially if you're using a lot of butter or spread.

Eat the corn on the cob a few rows at a time. Go light on the amount of butter you use to avoid too much butter dripping. Use your napkin frequently to wipe your mouth and chin.

**ESCARGOT:** Hold the escargot shell with the claw holder and remove and eat the escargot meat with the cocktail fork.

**GRAPEFRUIT:** A grapefruit is usually served with the seeds already removed and segments separated. Use a grapefruit spoon (serrated edged on the spoon bowl) to remove the segments. Start at the outer edge of the white pith (do not scoop the pith) and scoop under the fruit of the grapefruit, towards the center.

**GRAPES: Seedless:** If the grapes are in a cluster, cut a section with the grape scissors (if provided) or break off with your fingers and place on your plate. Eat grapes one at a time with your fingers. **With Seeds:** Eat like seedless grapes as above. Discretely remove the seeds with your fork or thumb and forefinger.

**HAMBURGER:** Always cut a hamburger in half before eating. Be careful not to load the hamburger with so many condiments that it becomes difficult to eat. You also can eat a hamburger with the fork and knife if it's too thick to eat with your hands.

**ICE CREAM:** Ice cream is at its best when softened. Set out to thaw until soft, but still holding its shape. A teaspoon is used for soft ice cream, while an ice cream fork (a combination of a fork and spoon) is used to eat sliced/firm ice cream.

**MEAT:** Unless in a casual setting, cut meat with your fork and knife. A serrated steak knife may be provided. Be careful not to cut into the top glazing of the china or porcelain plate. *Do not gnaw on the bones.* For boneless meat, use the fork and knife (serrated).

**OLIVES:** Eaten with either your fingers (casual) or a fork (formal) depending on how formal the event. Watch for pits.

**PAPAYA:** Papaya is served in halves and eaten with a spoon.

**PASTA:** It is not necessary to cut penne or ziti pasta into pieces before eating. (see Spaghetti section, page 111)

**PICKLES:** Generally considered a finger food. Cut large pickles with a fork and knife. Eat small pickles with fingers or a fork.

**PIZZA, CASUAL:** Eat pizza in a casual setting with your hands. Some prefer to fold the pizza slice towards the center (lengthwise) to keep the pizza toppings in place.

**PIZZA, FORMAL:** Although rarely served, individual pizzas may be served at more formal meals. Use the fork and knife to eat rather than your hands even though it may seem less fun.

**POTATOES, BAKED:** Eat a baked potato with a fork and knife only. It's acceptable to eat the skin on the bake potato.

**POTATOES, FRIED:** Unless in a casual setting, use your fork. Do not pick up greasy French fries with your fingers. For large fried potatoes, use a fork (and knife) only.

**POTATO SKINS:** Some potato skins look like they can be eaten with the fingers. However, whether the skins are fried or baked, use your fork and knife.

**SANDWICH, LARGE:** Always cut a large sandwich in half before eating. Cutting a square sandwich at a diagonal can make it easier to eat. Take small bites to keep the sandwich ingredients from spilling over. The large sandwich may also be eaten with fork and knife.

## SEAFOOD

**CLAMS, FRIED:** In a casual setting, eat fried clams with your fingers; in a formal setting, eat with a fork and knife.

**CRAB, WHOLE:** Use a lobster/crab cracker or nutcracker to crack the crab claws and hard shells. Use a cocktail fork to retrieve the crabmeat. To make it easier for your guests, have your fishmonger crack and prepare the whole crab.

**CRAB, SOFT-SHELL:** Eat a soft-shell crab with a regular fork (not cocktail) and knife. The soft outer shell is edible.

**LOBSTER TAIL:** Use a cocktail fork to retrieve the meat from the shell. Cut large pieces of lobster with your knife.

**MUSSELS:** Use the cocktail fork to eat mussels.

**OYSTERS OR CLAMS ON THE HALF SHELL:** Use a cocktail fork to eat oysters or clams on the half shell. Do not cut the oyster or clam. The liquid may be drunk from the half shell.

**SEAFOOD, FRIED:** Eat fried seafood with a fork and knife, unless served in small bite-size pieces. Eat fried fish with your fingers only in very casual settings.

**SHRIMP WITH SHELL:** In a casual setting, peel the shell off first and eat the shrimp meat with your fingers. For shrimp without a shell, use a fork and knife.

**SHRIMP WITH TAIL SHELL:** Eat with a fork and a knife for a formal event, or with your fingers if a casual meal. For casual meals, use the tail shell as the holder.

**SORBET:** Sorbet means sherbet. A sorbet is served to help *cleanse the palate* and to prepare the palate for the next course. Small servings of sorbet are often served after a highly flavorful dish(s). Sorbet is generally served in a small bowl with a small spoon or teaspoon. Don't confuse sorbet for a small dessert.

**SPAGHETTI:** How to eat spaghetti is one of the most frequently asked questions I receive at seminars, so obviously spaghetti is served often at business entertaining events.

The proper way to eat spaghetti is to twirl the spaghetti around your fork. *The secret is to start with only a few strands.* Be careful with long spaghetti because the more you twirl it, the bigger it gets. If it gets too big on the fork, slide it off the fork and start over.

The experts are able to twirl spaghetti just using a fork. Most people, however, use a large spoon or the rim of the plate, to help twirl the spaghetti onto the fork. Place the tines against the inside of the bowl of the spoon and twirl. Slightly angle the spoon to help push the strands around the fork.

The biggest problem with eating spaghetti is not in twirling, but in the thickness of the sauce; thin sauce does not stick to the pasta.

If you're struggling with twirling the spaghetti, I think it looks more dignified to cut the spaghetti. Although cutting spaghetti is not an approved method of eating spaghetti, it's better than pushing stray strands into your mouth or getting sauce all over your face.

If you have a choice in ordering pasta and are not good at twirling spaghetti, order ziti, macaroni or penne rather than risk the awkwardness of eating spaghetti. Smaller pasta is easier to eat.

If you really want to learn to eat spaghetti properly, practice at home using a commercially canned spaghetti and sauce. The commercial sauce is really thick and adheres to the spaghetti making it easy to twirl.

**SUSHI:** The popularity of sushi is growing our culture. Every savvy business person should learn how to order and eat sushi.

The basis of sushi is sticky rice, which is rice seasoned with rice wine vinegar. Sushi offers rice and vegetable combinations, and cooked or raw fish with rice and vegetable combinations. Most sushi bars also offer teriyaki and tempura.

**Nigiri** (na-gar-ee)
Hand-pressed sushi. A piece of fish placed on a ball of the sticky rice.

**Maki** (ma-key) **Nori** (Nor ee)
Sushi rolled in a thin layer of dried seaweed (nori) and cut into circular pieces. Maki may also be called nori maki. Traditionally, an order of maki is six to eight pieces.

**Sashimi** (sha-she-me)
Sashimi is thin slices of fine quality fish (raw or cooked).

**Wasabi** (wa-sa-bee)
Wasabi is Japanese horseradish, which is used to flavor the soy sauce. Wasabi is hot (in flavor), so use small amounts until you find the desired taste.

**Gari** (gar-ee)
Pickled ginger slices are used to cleanse the palate between different courses (or pieces) of sushi.

**Teriyaki** (ter-e-ah-key)
Meat or fish, which is grilled or broiled, is generally accompanied by a mild or sweet teriyaki sauce.

**Tempura** (tem-pur-a)
Vegetables or fish dipped in a light batter and deep-fried.

# HOW TO ORDER SUSHI

When ordering sushi, especially if you new to sushi, either order from the menu or ask the sushi chef for his advice.

## HOW TO EAT:
Sushi is meant to be eaten with the fingers, although some prefer to eat sushi with chopsticks.

**Step 1.** If you are eating sushi with your hands, be sure to cleanse your hands first.

**Step 2.** Place a small amount of soy sauce in the small container at your place setting. Mix a small amount of wasabi into the soy sauce. Start with small portions of soy sauce and add the wasabi to develop the most desired flavor. You can always add more soy sauce or wasabi, but you cannot subtract.

**Step 3.** If eating with your hands, pick up the sushi between your thumb and the middle finger with your index finger on top.

**Step 4.** Dip the *fish side* into the soy-wasabi mixture rather than the rice side. Dipping the rice side into the soy sauce can cause the rice to fall apart.

**Step 5.** Typically nigiri takes two bites and maki takes one. If there is a second bite, dip into the soy sauce mixture again and eat.

**Step 6.** Eat a piece of gari to refresh the palate for the next dish or course of sushi.

# HOW TO USE CHOPSTICKS

## How to Hold:
- Hold the first chopstick between your thumb and index finger.

- Hold the second chopstick as you would hold a pencil.

- Keep tips of chopsticks even and of the same length.

- Keep the lower chopstick stationary. Only the upper chopstick should pivot.

- Hold towards the back end (thicker end) rather than in the middle or close to the tip or front end (thinner end).

## Do:
- Do use the back ends (not the tips) of the chopsticks to retrieve food from a shared dish to place on your own plate.
- Do moisten the tips of the chopsticks with liquid such as soy sauce before starting. Do not moisten the tips of the chopsticks with your mouth.
- Do place chopsticks halfway in the original wrapper and fold the wrapper in half (over the tips of the chopsticks) when through using. This indicates the chopsticks are used.
- Do place with tips of chopsticks facing left when resting, when you are finished, or anytime you are not using the chopsticks.

## Do Not:
- Do not pass food to someone else with your chopsticks.
- Do not put the back end of the chopstick in your mouth.
- Do not point at anyone or anything with chopsticks.
- Do not stick a chopstick into the food or rice.
- Do not gesture with your chopstick.
- Do not touch or move the plates with chopsticks.
- Do not play with chopsticks.

# Section II: Dining Protocol

# H. TIPPING

*"The guidelines and expectations for tipping are as varied as the motives of the tipper."*

# TIPPING

Today, the expectation of a generous tip is the norm. However, tipping is actually an arbitrary gift rather than a guarantee. The tip will vary due to the type and quality of service, the region, and the value system of the tipper.

The following are guidelines for tipping based on an average level of service. Some may tip more or less depending on the service received. For the smaller tips, be prepared; bring small bills.

## HOTEL

### Doorman                                    $1+ per bag
The doorman may also help with transportation or with directions. Additional services may warrant an additional tip.

### Bellman                                    $1+ per bag
In addition to the luggage, the bellman may also help with getting ice, adjusting the room temperature, and setting up the luggage, all which warrant an additional tip.

### Maid                                       $1-$5 day
The cleaning staff is tipped based on room size, the length of your stay, and the quality of service. Tip everyday, not upon checkout.

### Room Service                              15-20 percent
In some hotels the room service gratuity is automatically added to the tab. If not, add the tip. Check your bill to verify if the tip has been added or not.

### Concierge                                 $5-$25++
The tip depends on the service and quality of the service. Concierges are valuable for helping with difficult-to-find reservations and tickets.

## DINING

The average dining tip ranges from 15–20 percent. Know that tips to the waiter are often split with the bus boy and other behind-the-scene helpers. Also, some restaurants will take a percentage of the larger tips to set aside for taxes. (see page 153)

Give more generous tips (20%+) at higher rated (four- and five-star) restaurants and resorts. Tipping on tax is a personal choice. If the food bill is $100 and the tax rate is 9%, a 20% tip will add $1.80 (tip on the tax) to the $20 tip for food. Total tip = $21.80.

**Owner**                                              **Do not tip**

**Maitre D' or Hostess**                                **$10++++**
The hostess or maitre d'hotel, who is the headwaiter, usually does not receive a tip unless a special service has been performed. Special services include getting you a prized table, moving you from an undesired location or helping with a special celebration or event. Depending on the service, there is no limit to the size of the tip.

**Receptionist/Host**                    **Tip may not be expected**
Some facilities will have a host or hostess greet you and help seat you. Alternatively, the host or hostess may be only in charge of reservations and will remain at the hostess station.

**The Server: Waiter or Waitress**              **15–20 percent**
Although 15% is the generally accepted tax rate, more are tipping 20% even at family-type restaurants.

**Sommelier**                    **15–20 percent of the wine tab**
The sommelier is often the manager of the wine assortment and selection. The sommelier can advise you on which type and which wine(s) to select based on the meal(s) you select and your budget.

The server generally prorates the tip to the sommelier so the guest only has to pay one tip on the total tab. Some guests may prefer to designate the server tip percentage and the sommelier tip percentage on the bill.

**Restroom Attendant**                                   **$1.00**
Some facilities will station an attendant in the restroom. Be sure to take some dollar bills or change when you go to "rest."

**Coat Check Attendant**                    **$1.00 per item**
Tip for checking outer garments, totes, packages, and other items.

**Parking Attendant**                          **$2.00-$3.00+**
The tip for parking and the tip for retrieving is paid each time you arrive or get your vehicle to leave. Any extra special requests or special parking of your new or prized vehicle warrants a higher tip. Tip when you give the keys and retrieve the keys.

**Valet**                     **$2.00-$3.00 retrieving the car**
                              **$1.00 for guarding the keys**
The valet may only be the guard of the keys while others behind the scene park and deliver the cars.

## TRAVEL AND BAG HANDLERS

Tips for a bag handler or a shuttle driver start at $1.00 per bag (if he or she helps with the luggage). Weather conditions or the distance the luggage is carried may also be factors in the tip amount.

Shuttles include any transportation from home or office to and from the airport (parking and terminal). For a short distance, such as the airport-parking shuttle, the tip may be only for bag handling.

A tip is given if the driver helps with the luggage:
**Parking Lot Shuttle**                              **$1 per bag**

**Rental Car Shuttle**                               **$1 per bag**

**Hotel Shuttle**                                          **$1 per bag**

**Door-to-door Shuttle**                          **$1 per bag**
For free shuttles provided by the facility or hotel, tip the driver for the luggage. For shuttles that charge for transportation, add 10 to 15 percent tip to the transportation costs. Luggage is extra.

**Skycap**                    **$1+ per bag (Airport or train)**
In addition to bag handling, the skycap may also help arrange for transportation, which will increase the amount of the tip.


## TRANSPORTATION

**Bus Driver**                              **Usually not tipped**
The bus driver is tipped if he or she helps with the luggage. The norm is $1 per bag.

**Taxi Driver**                              **12–15 percent**
Sometimes the tip is simply rounding up the fare to an even amount. Rather than counting out the tip or waiting for change from the driver, the taxi passengers often pay more or less than 15 percent just to get out of the taxi faster.

**Limousine Driver**                        **15–20 percent**
When making your own arrangements with the limousine company, ask what the company recommends for a gratuity percentage. Most will start at 15 percent, but those that excel in service are usually tipped 20 percent (or more).

Tipping factors include: the quality, condition and cleanliness of the vehicle, the manners and dress of the driver, the attention to the road, "extras" such as the latest newspapers or magazines, available beverages, unscheduled stop(s), extra help with the luggage, a longer-than-expected wait at the airport, or even driving in inclement weather.

For corporate transportation of multiple trips for an event or for an executive contract, the gratuity is generally guaranteed in the contract arrangements and is included in the master billing. However, some passengers will tip an additional amount for exceptional service, safe driving during bad weather conditions, additional help with luggage, or other special services.

# Section III

# FREQUENTLY ASKED QUESTIONS

The following questions were asked during protocol training
sessions conducted by Pat Mayfield Consulting, LLC.
The questions are in alphabetical order by topic.

*"Questions serve to gain and give information,
to quiz, to challenge, and to enlighten. Quality
questions are more apt to yield quality information."*

# FREQUENTLY ASKED QUESTIONS

## ACCESSORIES: Purses

**Q:** *When dining out, where do I put my purse during the meal? I've been told never to put my purse on the floor.*

**A:** Sometimes the floor is the only place available. Never put your purse, regardless of size, on the table or on the back of the chair. Purses do not belong on the dining or meeting table. Place your purse under the table in front of you, close to your feet so you know it is there.

If you place the purse to the side of the chair, someone might trip over it. If you place a purse on the back of the chair, it may be stolen or a passer-by might bump into it.

**Q:** *I take a small purse to formal events—too small to put on the floor.*

**A:** Place on your lap (under your napkin) and not on the floor. Select a purse that will not snag the fabric of your outfit.

## ACCESSORIES: Satchels and Briefcases

**Q:** *My daughter will be graduating in a few months and needs advice on the type of briefcase or satchel she should buy.*

**A:** She should select accessories that match her type of work. The more professional the profession, the more professional the accessories should be. Invest in classic, multi-purpose satchels and totes that are basic and always in style. Invest in the best quality she can afford. Also, she may find she will need an assortment of satchels or briefcases for different types of business meetings.

## ACCESSORIES: Writing Implements

**Q:** *Do I really need to invest in an expensive pen?*

**A:** It depends on the type of work you do. I have a branded roller-ball pen (my second in many years). Not only is this an image pen, I also really like using it.

If you are working in high-level business, invest in a pen and pencil you enjoy using as well as one that reflects the appropriate image of you and your profession.

## ACCESSORIES: When to Replace

**Q:** *I have a favorite briefcase. Because I've been in business a long time, the leather has worn off from some of the corners and edges. This briefcase has many memories for me and I believe the worn look adds to my look of expertise and experience.*

**A:** As time wears on, so do our business accessories. Don't wait too long before replacing. This question of broken-in versus new accessories has been raised numerous times.

We really can get attached to our tangible support system— sometimes too attached. Would you wear worn-out shoes to a meeting because they were your favorite pair? It's doubtful, regardless of how attached you are.

A good compromise is to replace the worn parts and keep the briefcase in good repair. However, sometimes the best option is to simply purchase a new briefcase with more updated features and improved materials.

## ANXIETY: Conquering Social Anxiety

**Q:** *I get really nervous when: 1) I have to go to a company event, and 2) when I'm hosting a business dinner. How can I become more comfortable at these events?*

**A:** 1) Determine which situations make you uncomfortable; your entrance to the event, introducing yourself, greeting others, dining manners, shaking hands, or carrying on a conversation. Once you have your list, start to work on improving the applicable areas.

Know that many people, regardless of title, rank or age, can be really nervous or uncomfortable at special events or dinners. Since most of us do not eat everyday in a formal manner, a formal meal can make even the most confident uncomfortable.

For some, speaking with one person can be as intimidating as speaking before a group. Join local clubs and associations to practice your conversational skills. Join a local Toastmasters Club to improve your speaking ability and to help overcome nervousness.

2) Think of the host as the leader and assume that leadership role. Practice is always a key to success, so eat out occasionally in upscale restaurants and practice being the host.

Take a trusted friend (not from your office) so you can play the part of host or hostess. Learn what's on the menu and how to pronounce the items. The waiter can help you with the selections and the pronunciations. Use the sommelier to help you order the wine. Practice the wine taste test with the help of the sommelier.

Improve your ability to review and pay the bill quickly and discretely. Remember—never let the guests see the bill.

**Q:** *Next month I will be attending my first national meeting of our company and I really dread it. I do not know how to talk to the executives without getting tongue-tied. How can I get over this?*

**A:** Many executives once felt just like you. They, too, found it hard to relax when meeting the leaders of the company. The greatest leaders are skilled in making those around them comfortable. Find a skilled networking mentor and observe what they say and do.

Here are some guidelines:

- Relax and be yourself. Take a few deep breaths (discretely) before you enter the room.

- Approach the event with a positive attitude. Understand that these meetings can be a real opportunity to observe your co-workers and the company executives outside the office. Use this time to fine tune your observation skills.

- Stand or sit up straight and hold your head high. When you look and act confidently, you actually will begin to feel more confident.

- Do your homework. Know the background of the leaders *before* you meet them. Asking them how they got started with the company, or if they have any advice for a new employee, may lead to an interesting, informative, and possibly revealing conversation.

- Do not try to dominate the conversation once you become more comfortable.

- Most of all become a great listener. We learn more from listening than we do from talking. Also, the more you listen, the less you have to talk.

## CHAIRS: Pushing In the Chair

**Q:** *I have a pet peeve about people not pushing their chairs in when they leave the table. Am I wrong?*

**A:** Pushing in the chair is the right thing to do. The table arrangement appears neater and it's also safer. No one will trip over a chair in its proper place.

## CHAIRS: When to Help

**Q:** *As a gentleman, should I help a lady with her chair at a business meeting or at a dining event?*

**A:** At a business meeting it is not appropriate, nor necessary, to help the woman get in or out of her chair, while at a social event, it is protocol and the courteous thing to do.

Regardless of whether it's business or not, if someone is struggling to get in or out of a chair, helping without fanfare is the thoughtful thing to do.

## CHAIRS: Where to Sit

**Q:** *Which chair should I sit in?*

**A:** Generally in business, rank sits by rank in order of rank. You usually are seated either across from or next to your counterparts. Guests should wait until the host asks them be seated. If the host does not indicate which chair, take the closest and most convenient seat to you, but pay attention to where those of rank are seated. A lower rank would not sit next to a higher rank unless asked.

# CLOTHING: Suits, Sports Coats, and Blazers★

**Q:** *I'm a guy who hates wearing coats. Is it acceptable to remove one's blazer or suit coat once seated at the dinner table?*

**A:** Do not take your blazer or jacket off. Keep it on through the entire meal (or meeting) unless:

1. The host or hostess suggests or encourages you to take your blazer, jacket, or suit coat off.

2. Your immediate supervisor takes his blazer off and says something to the effect of "Why don't we all be comfortable and take our jackets off."

Even if the highest-ranking person in the room removes his jacket, watch what your immediate supervisor does. Your direct line of command is the one to follow. When in doubt, keep your jacket on. Rarely would a man take his jacket off during a formal meal or event.

★*A dinner jacket is the most formal attire (tuxedo), although some refer to the jacket he wears to a formal dinner as his dinner jacket.*

*A suit coat, which matches the slacks, is either single- or double-breasted. A suit is considered dressier than a pair of slacks with a blazer, sports coat or jacket.*

*A blazer, sports coat or sport jacket is a dress coat or jacket made of different fabric or color than the slacks or pants. The term "sport" does not refer to an actual sport, but indicates a more casual than formal attire. A blazer is typically a solid navy blue or a solid black jacket.*

**Q:** *If it is sweltering hot and all the men are sweating, can we remove our jackets?*

**A:** No, not unless the host (or your superior) has given you permission or encouragement as discussed in the previous question. For hot weather, wear a lighter-weight suit or jacket. Wear a good cotton tee shirt underneath your dress shirt to avoid sweating through your shirt. Be sure to use antiperspirant or deodorant. Never let them see you sweat!

**Q:** *Since I rarely wear a suit or sports jacket I feel uncomfortable when I do. I really feel miserable in a tuxedo.*

**A:** In our culture of business casual today, many men and women are uncomfortable getting dressed up. For those who have high aspirations, the ability to be comfortable in dress clothes is necessary and important for those high-level meetings.

When a person is uncomfortable in his clothing, it shows. A man will tug at his collar or cuffs, and will shift around uncomfortably. Anytime you know you'll be uncomfortable in your clothing, put on the attire and wear at home for a while until you feel at ease.

**Q:** *Am I supposed to keep my dress jacket buttoned?*

**A:** Keep the jacket buttoned while standing. (For a three-button jacket, button at least the middle button.) If your jacket, whether single- or double-breasted, does not lay smooth when you are seated, you may unbutton the jacket when you sit down. Button the jacket back up with the appropriate buttons when you stand.

## CLOTHING: Outer Jackets, Coats, and Scarves

**Q:** *If there is no coat check and I have my jacket or long coat at the table, what is the best way to place it on my chair? And what do I do with my long scarf?*

**A:** Having lived in cold winter climates for many years, here's the system I use for a long jacket or heavy coat if there is not a coat check. This system keeps the jacket or coat off the floor, takes little space and has a neat appearance.

1. Stand behind the chair.

2. Take the jacket or coat by the shoulders (one hand on each shoulder) and hold slightly above the seat of the chair.

3. Lower or place the bottom of the coat down <u>the front</u> of the back of the chair.

4. Lower the bottom of the coat until the hem just touches the seat of the chair.

5. Lower (drape) the jacket or coat down <u>the back</u> of the chair and drape the shoulders of the coat over the top of the chair.

6. Gravity takes hold and the coat will naturally fall until the shoulder of the coat reaches the top of the back of the chair and the bulk of the coat drapes behind the chair.

**Scarves:** Fold and place a long scarf through one sleeve of the coat. You may need to fold the scarf so it will not touch the floor. Some scarves can be folded neatly and placed in a briefcase or purse.

**Q:** *Do I have to check my coat? It takes forever to stand in line and retrieve it after the event.*

**A:** At large or formal gatherings, you may wish to check you coat, hat and scarf. Even if it takes longer to retrieve the coat at the end of the event, you will appear more professional if you are not dragging a coat and hat around.

A gentleman will offer to check a female companion's (or female colleague) jacket or coat. Remember to tip the coat checker.

**Q:** *I'm a lady who feels uncomfortable when I have to check my own coat at a big event. Do you have any suggestions?*

**A:** The key is not to show that you are uncomfortable. Take it in stride; checking your coat is better than being the only woman dragging her coat around all evening.

As for feeling uncomfortable, act and feel like you belong. In business and social events today, many women and men are unescorted. The more comfortable you are with attending alone, the more you will enjoy the event.

**Q:** *What do I do with a dripping wet raincoat when there is no coat check? And, where do I put the wet umbrella?*

**A:** Because of liability issues, facilities do not want water drips on the floor and will make arrangements for the wet coats and umbrellas. Most facilities will have a coat rack available, even if it's not in view. Ask the manager or server where you might hang your coat. Hang the umbrella with your coat or place in the umbrella stand, if provided. Some facilities have plastic sleeves for wet umbrellas to help prevent dripping.

## CLOTHING: Caps, Hats, and Ties

**Q:** *Any problem with wearing a cap when I have a bad hair day?*

**A:** Yes, that can be a problem. Caps or hats (for men) are not to be worn inside; remove it when you enter the room. Do not wear a hat at the dining table, or in class or other meetings. Set your alarm clock early enough to do your hair.

Ladies may wear hats inside and at the table, especially in social settings. However, it is rare to see a woman wearing a hat during a business meeting today.

**Q:** *Can I tuck my tie in my shirt during the meal?*

**A:** Do not tuck the tie in your shirt. If you bring the food to your face, rather than your face to the food, you are less likely to get your tie in the food. The solution to keeping a clean tie is to sit up straight, do not dribble food (take smaller bites), and be careful when eating soup, chili, gravy or sauces that can splatter, such as spaghetti or marinara sauce.

**Q:** *Can I loosen my tie in a casual meeting?*

**A:** It depends on the setting. The loosened tie is more than just a casual look—it's an unkempt look. Men loosen their tie when they are through working, so the image is not so much of getting down to work, as the work *is over*.

It's best to remove your tie completely and place in your briefcase or jacket pocket. Always follow the example of the higher-ranked males in the room.

## CLOTHING: Taking Shoes Off

**Q:** *I understand my boss asks his guests to remove their shoes when they come to his home. Is this proper and do I have to do this? We're invited to a party at his house next month.*

**A:** Removing shoes in someone's home is not the norm in our culture. Even though removing shoes in one's home is practiced, this practice may not be honored during social events.

But if the boss wants everyone to remove his or her shoes, unless you have a substantial reason not to, just do it. The good news is that you've been alerted.

People ask guests to remove their shoes before entering the home for a variety of reasons, including their culture, and the desire to reduce the amount of dust, dirt, and other allergens coming into the house. The key is to be prepared; make sure you have clean socks, socks without holes, hose without runs, and clean and groomed feet. Better to have something covering your feet rather than to walk around barefooted.

## CLOTHING: Type of Shoes

**Q:** *I'm a lady who loves to wear open-toe and sling (open back) shoes. Are these shoes proper for business?*

**A:** For the more serious and professional appearance one should wear closed-toe pumps. Save the "open-anything" shoes for social events. However, open-toe and sling shoes are fashionable and fun, so just think about the image you want to portray. In some industries, fashionable shoes would be preferable.

## CORRESPONDENCE: Writing Notes

**Q:** *Any advice for writing thank you notes?*

**A:** Try to be creative rather than write the canned thank you note. Be specific rather than general as to why you are thanking the person. Also, the use of too many "I's" puts the focus on you; a thank you note is about them, not you.

**Canned:** (Note the overuse of "I's")
*I want to thank you for the lovely evening. I had a really good time. The dinner was delicious. I really enjoyed meeting your family. Thanks again.*

**Creative:** (Note not one "I" is used)
*What a wonderful dinner! The homemade pasta with the artichokes was a wonderful combination. The apple pie was especially enjoyable as the pie reminded me of special times shared around the table back home. The warm hospitality of your family made me feel so welcome. Thank you for a memorable evening.*

## CORRESPONDENCE: Stationery

**Q:** *What kind of "note" stationery do you use?*

**A:** I like to use correspondence cards and medium-size, fold-over cards. Both measure close to 6½ by 4½ inches. I also use smaller size fold-over notes for shorter messages. For both sizes, matching envelopes with the printed return address give a professional look.

To personalize your stationery, a correspondence card may have your name or initials across the top of the card. Some may also add the address across the bottom. Fold-over notes can have the name, initials or logo on the front fold.

## DEFINITIONS: Host and No Host Bar

**Q:** *What is a hosted bar, no-host bar, cash bar, and open bar?*

**A:** In a no-host or cash bar, the guests purchase their drinks and tip the bartender. Some hosts will pay for sodas or water, while the guests pay for the alcoholic beverages.

In a hosted or open bar, the host picks up the tab and the tip.

## DEFINITIONS: Faux Pas

**Q:** *What is a faux pas?*

**A:** French for "you messed up" (or "false step"). A faux pas is a social mistake. The pronunciation is *foe-pah*.

## DEFINITIONS: RSVP

**Q:** *What does RSVP mean?*

**A:** RSVP is from the French phrase *repondez s'il vous plait,* which means *please reply*. Since RSVP includes "please," one would not extend an invitation with Please RSVP—just RSVP.

## DEFINITIONS: Soup de jour

**Q:** *What does soup de jour mean?*

**A:** De jour means *of the day*. Soup or other food dishes may be on the menu as the "de jour" dish featured by the restaurant that day.

## DEFINITIONS: Filet and Fillet

**Q:** *What's the difference between a filet and a fillet ?*

**A:** A filet of steak is pronounced fil-lay; a thin boneless strip of fish is called a fillet and is pronounced fill-it.

## ACCOMMODATING GUESTS WITH DISABILITIES

**Q:** *What are some suggestions for accommodating guests with disabilities?*

**A:** The following are some suggestions and guidelines:

- When referring to guests with disabilities, refer to the person first, then the disability. Always use *person first* terminology, such as:
    - A person who has a disability
    - A person who is blind or visually impaired
    - A person who uses a wheelchair
    - A person who is deaf or hard of hearing

- When introducing yourself, directly face the person who is visually impaired or blind. Let them know when you leave or are moving away from them.

- Talk directly to the person who is deaf or hard of hearing rather than their companion or sign-language interpreter.

- Assist a person who is visually impaired or blind by explaining the arrangement of the tableware and describing the placement of food and beverage items as they are served using the face of a clock. For example, "Your meat is at 6 o'clock and your vegetables are at 3 o'clock."

- Do not touch or lean on a person's wheelchair.

- Do not use the term "handicap." Handicap has a negative meaning to persons with disabilities.

- Parking for persons with disabilities is "Accessibility Parking" and is no longer called "Handicapped Parking."

- When speaking with a person who reads lips, talk slowly and do not cover your mouth, which would block the person's ability to read your lips clearly.

- Always ask before offering to help someone with a disability. If he or she declines your offer, please do not be offended. Do not pet a service animal or guide dog because it would distract or disorient the animal from their duties.

## ENTERTAINING: Paying the Bill

**Q:** *I'm new in my position and will be responsible for entertaining clients. What's the best way to pay the dining bill?*

**A:** The polished professional pays the tab (bill) discretely, quickly, and without fanfare. Here are just a few guidelines: He or she who invites, pays. Always review the bill for accuracy. Add the gratuity as quickly and discretely as you can. Before you arrive, make sure you have your credit card and that it is valid.

If you think there might be a hassle over who pays the bill, you can give your credit card to the waiter before the meal, tell him what gratuity percentage to add and have him bring you the completed receipt at the end. That prevents any hassle over who pays, especially if you are a businesswoman entertaining gentlemen who still have a hard time with a lady picking up the tab.

If you have never had the entertaining responsibility of a host, practice by dining at moderately priced restaurants; this will help you to get the experience of being the host and paying the tab.

You do not have to eat out to practice paying bill and tip. Practice adding the different tip percentages, e.g. 15% and 20% to different amounts of a bill *before* you go to the restaurant (see page 153).

Go to at least one fine restaurant, even if it's for lunch, to get the experience of the four- or five-star restaurant. The more you dine in upscale restaurants, the more confident and comfortable you will feel as the host in formal situations.

The number-one rule is to make your guests feel comfortable. This is critical—the more comfortable you are, the more you will put your guests at ease.

## FOOD: Food-to-Face

**Q:** *Is it acceptable to bend down close to the plate to eat? I spill less food that way.*

**A:** I call this the *food-to-face* or *face-to-food* question. We have become so casual in our dining habits in the past years that diners actually are unsure if placing their face close to the food plate is right or wrong.

Just remember, it's always *food to the face*. Keep your posture straight and bring the food to you. Avoid the appearance of diving into your food as in eating from a trough. Not a pretty sight!

If you have the *face-in-food* habit, force yourself to eat properly when you're among friends, at home or alone. Only practice will change or break this habit and this is a habit anyone in business will want to break.

## FOOD: Soup and Sherry

**Q:** *Recently I ordered a crab soup and a small container of sherry was served with the soup. I wasn't sure what to do with it. Why did they give me sherry?*

**A:** Sherry, a wine with a nutty flavor, is often added to a soup just before the soup is eaten. Typically, sherry is added to crab, turtle, or lobster soup or stew.

You can choose if you want to add the sherry or not. It is optional. Note: anytime you are not sure about what you've been served or what's on the menu, know that you can always ask the server.

## FOOD: Bread

**Q:** *At home, I always sop my bread in the sauce or gravy so I don't miss a bite. Is there anything wrong with this?*

**A:** When you're in public, it may be better to forgo that last drop of the sauce or gravy. Sopping the bread is not acceptable in our culture, especially when dining out—and especially in business. If you have the habit of sopping or cleaning your plate with a piece of bread, I strongly encourage you to break this habit.

However, in some fine restaurants, the chef might be disappointed if you leave any of his or her fabulous sauce on the plate. So, if you feel you must, tear off a small piece of the bread, pierce it with your fork, and then absorb (not swipe) the sauce with the bread that's on your fork. It's more dignified. Avoid "cleaning" your plate with bread.

When in doubt, don't. Take your cue from your host or hostess.

**Q:** *Aren't we supposed to "sop" bread in the olive oil and spice mixture at an Italian restaurant?*

**A:** Yes, and you would hold the bread (broken into a bite-size piece) with your hands. Sometimes the facility will provide balsamic vinegar to mix with the olive oil.

**Q:** *How am I supposed to eat the bread served as a bread soup bowl—the round hollowed bread?*

**A:** If you eat all the soup, you can use your fork and knife to cut pieces of the bread to eat. One would not cut the bread if the soup would pour out. Do not feel obligated to eat the bread. In some cases, the bread is simply a fun serving container.

## FOOD: Sharing with Others

**Q:** *Our team goes out a lot and we always share food from each others plates (not family-style service from platters). Anything wrong with this?*

**A:** It sounds like your group is a close-knit team, so my answer probably won't make any difference to you. However, the general rule is not to share food no matter how much you would like to, especially in business situations.

Some are quite averse to sharing food—including desserts—with anyone. Others may be germ phobic and do not want to be close or touch another person's germs. When someone says he does not want to share, believe him. Respect resistance.

Desserts are often ordered with additional forks or spoons for sharing. Tasting one or two bites of the "community dessert" is common, but not necessarily appropriate.

**Q:** *What do I say if someone offers to share food, but I don't want to?*

**A:** Simply say "No, thank you."

**Q:** *What if my new boss insists that I taste a bite of his food?*

**A:** Plan A: Take a small bite and say, "Thank you."
Plan B: (See Plan A)

## FOOD: Toothpicks

**Q:** *If the restaurant provides toothpicks with the meal or on the counter, is it acceptable to use one?*

**A:** Yes, but not in public. *Never* in public.

## FOOD: Chewing Ice

**Q:** *I love to chew ice. Any problem?*

**A:** Yes. Don't chew ice at the table or in public. Ice chewing is noisy and usually people who chew ice chomp noisily.

## FOOD: Salt and Pepper Shakers

**Q:** *Which holder is for the salt and which is for the pepper?*

**A:** This can be a problem. One may not know if it's salt *or* pepper in an unmarked opaque shaker. Some place salt in the shaker with smaller holes because it slows the flow, while others place salt in the shaker with larger holes because they want the salt to pour freely.

Always test the shakers first. When in doubt, tap (once) on your plate (not on your wrist or palm) to see if it is salt or pepper.

Today, I serve salt and pepper in see-through shakers. That avoids any question about what's inside.

## HOLIDAYS: Gift Giving

**Q:** *I'm new to my job. Am I expected to give my boss a gift for the holidays?*

**A:** *The rule is that you never give "up" to supervisors or even further up the ladder.*

However, here are the challenges to the rule:
1. Some bosses like to receive gifts.
2. Some bosses expect to receive gifts.

Since you are new at this company, ask co-workers (more than one) what the company policy or tradition is on gift giving. You may also want to ask what they gave the boss last year.

If you decided to give a gift, be wise.
1. Keep it simple. Do not give an extravagant gift.
2. Avoid anything that is too personal or intimate.
3. Save the funny gifts for your personal friends.
4. Avoid gift certificates.
5. Never give cash.

## HOLIDAYS: Company Parties

**Q:** *I hate to attend the annual company holiday party. How can I get out of it gracefully?*

**A:** Unfortunately, unless you are seriously ill or have a personal emergency, you should attend. It is often noticed more if people do not show up than when they do. Office holiday parties are given to build morale and pay tribute to the employees. Take the time to go and get to know your colleagues better. Remember that one of the keys to success is simply showing up—even if it's a holiday party.

## HOLIDAYS: Holiday Cards

**Q:** *Do I really need to send holiday cards for my business? I just have no time this year.*

**A:** As unimportant as you might think holiday cards are, some companies actually keep track of who sends and who does not. I encourage you, whether you are a vendor, client or customer, to make a special effort to take the time to send holiday greetings.

Holiday cards are a symbol of caring. Most people enjoy receiving cards, especially cards with a personal touch. Be thoughtful. Kind words and actions can be the best gifts of all.

Add a handwritten note on any pre-printed cards. Please do not use e-mail messages as a substitute for a holiday card. E-mail messages look weird sitting on the mantle.

As convenient as electronic cards are, the electronic card does not carry the same impact as the mailed card. Also, initially all electronic greeting cards were free, so other than taking a few seconds to create and send there is no dollar and time or effort investment of the sender.

A Thanksgiving card is especially a thoughtful card for business. In addition to being a card specific to thanks, it's also a card at the start of the holiday season. Another reason to send Thanksgiving cards is that since so few do, you diversify yourself.

It's my opinion that New Year's greeting cards do not have the same impact as other end-of-the-year holiday cards because people are actually winding down from the holidays. Many are putting up the decorations when the card arrives. However, depending on the card, some New Year's cards can help welcome the year.

## INTERVIEWING: Basic Manners

**Q:** *I'm getting ready to enter the job market. What are the basic manners in interviews?*

**A:** Here are a few interview guidelines:
- Wait for the interviewer to offer you a chair before you sit down. Some may gesture for you to be seated.

- If asked if you would like something to drink, accept the offer, even if you've already had five cups of coffee.

- Use the courtesy titles "Mr." or "Ms." until the interviewer asks you to call them by his or her first name. Unless you've already talked with him or her (telephone interview or personal meeting) on a first name basis, wait for permission.

- Send a handwritten thank you note within 24 hours. Write to your main contact or the person who interviewed you, or both.

## INTERVIEWING: Overcoming Nervousness

**Q:** *How can I get over nervousness when I go on an interview?*

**A:** You are not alone. Interviews are important and most people are nervous during an interview.

- Be thoroughly prepared. Have a perfectly written resume and do not forget to bring extra copies with you.
- Make and take a list of questions you will ask—remember you are interviewing the interviewers as well.
- Practice before the interview. Set up a mock interviewing session. Get in front of a mirror. Use a tape recorder or a video camera to tape the session.
- Relax. Always have a plan B and C. People are more relaxed when they believe they have alternative options.

## INTERVIEWING: Dress

**Q:** *How many interviewing "power" outfits for a woman are needed?*

**A:** Someone once told me she believed she did not get a job because she was not as well dressed for the second interview as she was for the first interview.

- Have at least two or three power outfits that make you feel confident and comfortable.

- Invest in separates and accessories that you can coordinate, or buy basic dresses with different jackets or blazers to create different looks.

- Ask the store for personal shopper assistance to help organize your interviewing wardrobe for appropriate (to the industry and company) accessories.

## INTERVIEWING: Summer Clothing

**Q:** *What do you recommend I wear during an interview in the hot summer? I wilt!*

**A:** That is a tough question. Winter clothes typically look more professional. The fabrics, however, can make a real difference in summer-interview clothing.

I recommend avoiding linen. Many love linen because it is a natural fiber, but linen wrinkles badly. Unless you are interviewing with someone who loves linen, you are just going to appear too wrinkled to the interviewer.

To beat the heat, wear a lightweight suit and stay in the air conditioning as much as possible. If you have a long walk to the interview, arrive early enough to cool down. Remember—never let them see you sweat!

## MEETINGS: Off-Site Meetings and Events

**Q:** *It is my impression off-site company events are supposed to be more relaxed and casual than office events. What is wrong with letting my guard down a bit? Is that not the real purpose of an off-site meeting?*

**A:** Off-site business events and meetings are business meetings, no matter how informal the event. Never let your guard down so much that you dip below the acceptable line of proper protocol.

How you act at off-site meetings is as important as your on-site behavior. There is a strong chance that you are being observed so make sure all you actions and comments pass the scrutiny test.

**Q:** *I feel I can dress down at company picnics. At the last annual picnic, I wore short-shorts and someone made a snide comment about my outfit. Wasn't he out of line?*

**A:** Unsolicited advice is rarely welcomed. To offer unsolicited advice can be (and generally is) out of line, but it depends on the method, motivation and intent. That person might have been saying to you what others were saying behind your back. The intention may have been more to help you than to harm you.

As hard as it was to hear the comment, the person may have done you a favor. Short shorts are rarely appropriate at company social events (unless specified in the dress code).

Remember that for an off-site company-sponsored event or an event (even a back-yard barbeque) at the home of a superior, the attire still has to be appropriate and acceptable. The key is to dress appropriately for the occasion and not be sloppy, provocative, suggestive, or too casual.

## MISCELLANEOUS: First Impressions

**Q:** *This is such a simple question, but what specifically is a good first impression?*

**A:** A person makes an impression in the first three to seven seconds. One's professional and personal imprint includes: 1) attire and appearance, 2) body language, 3) attitude, actions and behavior, and 4) smell.

For a good first impression:
- Be appropriately dressed and groomed.
- Have a positive attitude and a cooperative spirit.
- Use appropriate body language.

- Be authentic and genuine. Be yourself.
- Use appropriate language. Use a pleasant tone.
- Avoid too much perfume or cologne. Avoid eating spicy foods or garlic 24 hours before the event.

## MISCELLANEOUS: Spit and Polish

**Q:** *I have a bad habit of spitting. As long as I'm outside, can't I spit?*

**A:** Spit: No.   Polish: Yes.

## MISCELLANEOUS: Sunglasses

**Q:** *Is it acceptable to wear sunglasses at an outdoor event? They cannot see my eyes if I do.*

**A:** My policy is to wear sunglasses in the glaring sun, but remove them while talking. Wear a hat or cap or move to the shade.

## MISCELLANEOUS: Smoking

**Q:** *I'm a smoker. When is it acceptable to smoke?*

**A:** In our culture, smoking is not as acceptable as it once was. If you have to smoke, find a designated smoking area.

Here is the problem with leaving the dining table or the meeting to smoke (or for any other reason):
- When a person leaves the group, he removes himself from the meeting and possibly from important discussion.
- If you are the only smoker in the group, you further separate yourself away from the group.

- If anyone in the group is allergic to smoke, the smell of smoke will remain on your clothing, your fingers and your breath, which may leave a negative imprint on the non-smoker(s).

If your smoking addiction is so strong that you just have to take a smoking break, be sure to:

- Try to leave during non-business discussion time. Leave for only a short time.

- If others are around, avoid blowing smoke in their direction.

- Wash your hands before returning to the meeting or dining table. Hands smell of tobacco after you've smoked.

- Take a breath mint before you return.

## MISCELLANEOUS: Outside the Office

**Q:** *Last week I took my family to a local restaurant. I noticed that my boss was there with a group. He appeared to be having some type of celebration. Should I have said hello to my boss?*

**A:** This is one of those *it depends* situations. It depends on your boss, your relationship with your boss, and the location.

Some bosses would expect you to come over and would be offended if you didn't. Unfortunately, some bosses would not want to be disturbed.

Risk A: If you go over and he would rather not be disturbed, he may be ticked off that you interrupted.

Risk B: If you do not go over and your boss has seen you there, he may wonder why you avoided him—or even worse, snubbed him.

Try to discretely get his or her attention through eye contact. If you can observe his or her body language response before you stop by, you will have a better feel of whether to go over or not.

*If you choose to stop by and say hello:*
- Be sure not to interrupt anyone's sentence.
- Be very brief and do not linger.
- If it is a celebration, such as a birthday party, then wish the person a happy birthday.
- Avoid asking questions, such as asking, "Is this your wife (or husband)" or other personal questions.
- Say how nice to see him, or that you wanted to say hello.


## MISCELLANEOUS: Handkerchief

**Q:** *Do I really need to carry a handkerchief with me? I never see anyone using them anymore.*

**A:** Handkerchiefs are great for sneezing and coughing. Some carry tissues with them, but tissues are harder for men to carry. Handkerchiefs are soft, foldable, and a godsend when needed.


## MISCELLANEOUS: Getting Into a Car

**Q:** *What is the proper way to get in and out of a car? I wear skirts above the knee and this can be awkward.*

**A:** Short skirts can really be a problem, and this is one of the reasons I recommend pant suits or longer skirts—especially if you are in situations that can be too revealing.

To get into a car, back into the seat with your knees together. If someone is holding the door for you, keep direct eye contact, which helps keep the eyes focused on the face. Lift your knees slightly, and then rotate your body in towards the car seat by turning the knees towards the front. Practice.

## MISCELLANEOUS: Seating Rank in the Car

**Q:** *Where does the highest-ranked person sit in a car?*

**A:** In the front passenger seat of a normal-size automobile if he or she is not driving. In a limousine, a window seat is preferred. Similar to an airplane, the window and aisle seats are the desired seats—not the middle seat.

## NETWORKING: Business Cards

**Q:** *You tell us to always have a business card available, but exchanging business cards at a gala or other black-tie event seems tacky to me.*

**A:** The theory is that one does not exchange business cards at formal "social" events even if the main connection of the event is business. The reality is that sometimes business cards are discretely exchanged at formal social events.

However, business cards are not exchanged at the table or during the meal. Business cards are exchanged only if a card is requested.

Do not ask a high-ranking executive for a card. If the executive wants to exchange cards, he or she will ask.

**Q:** *I'm new to networking. When is the right time to give my business card to someone I just met?*

**A:** Take time to visit with someone before asking for a card. Giving out a card quickly reveals one's eagerness, which shows: inexperience, poor manners, or a lack of knowledge or respect.

**Q:** *What do I do with my business cards when I am at a networking event? Do I carry the cards in my hand?*

**A:** Keep cards in a pocket, wallet or side pocket of your satchel or purse. Use a business card case when possible. Do not keep your business cards in your hand ready for the exchange. You would appear too eager.

### NETWORKING: Food

**Q:** *You tell us not to eat and drink at the same time while we are networking. But what if we are hungry and need to eat?*

**A:** At true networking events where you are expected to meet and greet others, you always want to have your right hand free for shaking hands. So that hand must be clean.

My personal reminder at these events is that *"It's not about the food."* This helps to remind me that a couple of tasty morsels are less important than properly greeting that someone special I have been waiting to meet.

The bottom line is that the food is just not worth it. Too many networking events serve messy and hard-to-eat finger foods, which each tidbit take two to three bites to eat. If your goal is to network,

Remember that you are there for meeting people at the event, not for the food or drink.

If you have to eat:
Plan A: If you are absolutely starving, get some food and eat. Wash and thoroughly dry your hands before returning to network. Take only a few minutes for this so you do not take yourself totally out of the event.

Plan B: Either eat or drink, but not at the same time. Use your left hand for eating or for holding the drink. Keep your right hand available and clean to shake hands. Eat only those tidbits that appear easy and quick to eat.

Plan C: Eat a light snack before you go or plan to treat yourself to a nice dinner following the event.

Another situation to avoid other than eating is chewing gum. Talking and chewing gum don't go together. Do not chew gum at the networking event.

## TIPPING: Bad Service

**Q:** *I was taught to leave a penny tip if someone gives bad service. Is that correct?*

**A:** The problem with leaving a penny is the waiter does not know whether you did not like the service, whether you are cheap, or whether you simply forgot your penny.

By leaving only a penny tip, you may or may not be sending a *meaningful* message to the waiter. A better way, if you have not been able to get through to your waiter, is to let the manager know *during* the meal that the service is unacceptable, not after the fact.

## TIPPING: Calculating the Tip

**Q:** *I freeze when I get the bill because I have a hard time figuring out the tip. How can I improve this?*

**A:** Calculating the tip is a challenge for many. Learn techniques that help you speed the process of calculating the tip. Here are three examples on the same bill: The food bill is $28.00 and the tax percentage (8%) is $2.24 for a total bill (or tab) of $30.24.

1) Odd numbers may be difficult to multiply by 15 percent in your head, so round the odd number up or down to the closest even number and multiply by 15 percent.

   The total bill is $30.24. This amount is easier to round down to $30.00. Multiply by 15% and the tip is <u>$4.50.</u>

2) Another way is to multiply by .10 (percent) and divide that number by two (which will give you the five percent).
   A) Multiply $30.24 by .10 = $3.02
   B) Divide the above ($3.02) by two = $1.51
   C) Add A) $3.02 plus B) $1.51 to reach the 15 percent tip = <u>$4.53</u>

3) If tax is 7.5 percent or more, simply double the tax that is already on the bill for a 15 percent tip.
   Food bill: $28.00
   Tax (8%): $ 2.24 <u>x's 2 = $4.48 tip</u>
   Total: $30.24

Notice how similar the tips are from the three calculations:
1 = $4.50    2 = $4.53   3 = $4.48

Learn to calculate the tip without a chart or calculator. Practice. Take different sums and determine the tip. Practice at home or the office until you know you can pay the bill quickly and comfortably.

## AIRPLANE MANNERS: What's Appropriate?

**Q:** *I recently traveled cross-country after many months of not traveling by air. I was surprised at the rudeness of the passengers. Do you have any suggestions on airplane manners?*

**A:** One of the biggest changes in airline travel is the size of the luggage and built-in wheels, which has enabled the passengers to bring more luggage on board. Now passengers compete—sometimes rudely—to get to the overhead bins first.

Here are a few guidelines:

- Know that all passengers have equal rights to the overhead bins, armrests, and any other shared space.

- Keep your feet covered. If you take your shoes off, put on socks or other foot coverings over your feet.

- Do not put your feet on the bulkhead or wall of the airplane. It's the same thing as putting your feet on someone's furniture.

- Do not place your feet (covered or not) on the armrest of the person in front of you.

- Do not put your "stuff" under *your seat*. That area belongs to the person behind you. Place your "stuff" *under the seat in front of you.*

- If you take food on the plane, try to avoid high aroma foods such as garlic-flavored foods, fish, or fried foods. The smells linger in the enclosed airplane.

- If you are rearranging the overhead bin, do not place objects on top of someone's coat. Find the owner of the coat (they're usually close by) and let them know you're moving it.

## About Pat Mayfield Consulting, LLC…

**METHODS:**
Consulting
Speeches and Seminars
Facilitation
Executive Coaching
Books and Articles

**SPECIALIZING IN:**
Sales
Negotiating
Customer Service
Leadership
Business Protocol

## About Pat…

PAT MAYFIELD is the president of Pat Mayfield Consulting, LLC, a business consulting and training company providing services to clients nation-wide. She is the author of five books and a co-author of five books. Her company offers consulting and training in both the private and public sectors, and in educational institutions.

Since starting her company in 2000, Pat has worked with hundreds of clients with successful results. Clients ranged from start ups to multibillion dollar clients. Pat frequently offers leadership training programs for executives, and facilitates retreats and meetings for Boards of Directors.

Prior to starting her own company, Pat was a national award-winning sales executive responsible for managing several multi-million dollar businesses. She successfully helped establish a multi-million dollar business in which she also created and managed the national sales force.

Her awards include being named one of the *"Top 25 Who Made It Happen"* in the furniture industry by *High Points* magazine, and the *National President's Award* from the Accessory Resource Team, the industry association, for developing a national retail education program.

She holds the following degrees:  BS from the University of Arkansas, MA from Columbia University, and MBA from St. Mary's College

For information on:
Seminars, training, speeches or facilitation, contact Pat at:

www.patmayfield.com

## Books by Pat Mayfield

*Giving and Getting: Tips on Negotiating*
*Business Tips and Techniques – The Collection*
*The Competitive Circle*
*Manners for Success*

## Co-Authored Books

*Leadership Defined*
Featuring General Alexander Haig, Alan Keys, and Dr. Warren Bennis

*Conversations on Success*
Featuring Stephen Covey, Dr. Denis Waitley, and Marjorie Blanchard

*Speaking of Faith*
Featuring Dr. Robert Schuller, Ann Jillian, and Dave Dravecky

*Getting Things Done*
A collection of interviews from 12 successful women

*Blue Prints for Success*
Featuring Stephen Covey and Ken Blanchard

## Video
*Challenging Foods*
A 13-minute video on eating difficult and challenging foods.